A MIND
Renewed
BY GOD

KIMBALL HODGE

D1016045

HARVEST HOUSE PUBLISHERS
Eugene, Oregon 97402

Cover by Koechel Peterson & Associates, Minneapolis, Minnesota

A MIND RENEWED BY GOD

Copyright © 1998 by Kimball Hodge
Published by Harvest House Publishers
Eugene, Oregon 97402

Library of Congress Cataloging-in-Publication Data

Hodge, Kimball, 1942–
    A mind renewed by god / Kimball Hodge
        p. cm.
    Includes biographical references.
    ISBN 1-56507-934-5
    1. Thought and thinking—Religious aspects—Christianity.   2. Christian life—Baptist authors.   I. Title.
    BV4598.4.H63   1998
    248.4—dc21   98-16022
                                                                                                          CIP

Printed in the United States of America

        98   99   00   01   02   03   / BO /   10   9   8   7   6   5   4   3   2   1

*To Lynda, my wife, who is God's gracious gift to me.
As my partner in life and ministry, you have
discovered and applied these principles with me.*

Acknowledgments

I wish to extend my heartfelt gratitude to the following:

Bob Hawkins, Sr.: For his kind encouragement to put these principles in print.

Steve Miller: For his indispensable and insightful guidance throughout the entire process of writing.

The congregations where these principles were developed and taught and for their enthusiastic response to these principles:

First Baptist Church of St. Cloud, Minnesota
Melrose Baptist Church of Oakland, California
Grace Baptist Church of Glendora, California

And a special thank you to the First Baptist Church of Eugene, Oregon, its staff, leaders, and people, who have prayed for and supported me in every way through the completion of this book.

Contents

Where Real Change Begins

The cold night air gnawed through her clothing as she pulled her tattered coat tightly around herself. She walked quickly through the darkness, not because of fear, but rather to stay ahead of the chill. Only a few dim lamps accompanied her silent walk along the familiar streets.

Her life had been a maze of troubling experiences for as long as she could remember. Her solitary walks were, for her, an escape from a squalid home and from the people who were related by blood while living as strangers to one another. Her father made his living as an innkeeper by day and as a petty thief by night. One moment he might be indulgent and the next abusive. Her mother, in her own attempt to survive, for the most part ignored her daughter and her needs. Most of the interaction between them as a family was punctuated with angry words and cursing.

That is why, after everyone else had fallen asleep, Eponine would quietly slip out into the night and take her lonely walk. Although no one seemed curious enough to ask her about her strange nightly ritual, if they had, she would probably have said that it was a time when she could be alone with her thoughts.

She had fallen in love with Marius, but he did not have the same feelings for her. Eponine described her actions by saying, "Sometimes I walk alone at night when everybody else is sleeping. I think of him and then I'm happy with the company I'm keeping. The city goes to bed and I can live inside my head."

The lonely young woman, as you may have recognized, is one of the characters in Victor Hugo's epic story of the French Revolution, called *Les Misérables*. She inhabits, with many others of Hugo's characters, a time of poverty and repression with little hope of ever experiencing true happiness. The only place she can find encouragement is somewhere inside her head in a world of her own making, where imagination rescues her from reality.

A number of years ago when I attended a musical performance of *Les Misérables,* Eponine's haunting solo struck a sympathetic chord in my soul. Of course, I cannot claim that my reality parallels hers. Not only do I live in a different time and place, but I also have not experienced either the poverty or abuse or hopelessness that were rampant in her world. Her words, however, kept pestering me and caused me to feel an affinity with her because she escaped her sadness by *living inside her head.*

My world of imagination developed very early in childhood. One of my first memories as a four-year-old was the separation of my parents and their ultimate divorce. The confusion of custody followed, with the eventual result being a long-term separation from my mother. About eight years after the split, I saw my mother for a few hours and then not again until I was twenty-eight years old.

Had you asked me, I would have said that because of the love of my father and grandparents, the separation didn't have much affect on me. I knew I was never angry with my parents for their divorce, but there were questions without answers and my childish mind rehearsed many of them in the privacy of my imagination.

I remember making up stories and songs about families and relationships, but as I did, something strange took place. Unlike Eponine, who designed for herself a world of happiness and love in the midst of hopelessness, I acted out my sense of loss in sad tales of discouragement.

It is not my purpose here to seek your pity or fill these pages with the details of a sad childhood story. Rather, I wish to share how God, in His gracious providence, grabbed my attention and dramatically changed the direction of my life.

As I moved into my teenage years and finally adulthood, a habitual pattern of thinking slowly emerged. My childish imaginations of sadness and loss formed the basis for my bouts with discouragement and even depression during my adult years.

Some people might have diagnosed my problem as a midlife crisis, but I was not yet in midlife when the crisis came. I had trained for ministry and was pastoring a church. I loved teaching God's Word, but struggled greatly with the dichotomy between the words of encouragement I spoke from the pulpit and the feelings of discouragement I regularly suffered from within.

The crisis finally came when I realized I could no longer teach one thing and live another. The answer seemed to be that I was not cut out to be a pastor or teacher.

Then God intervened. He began by setting me on a search through Scripture to discover the answers to my questions. He also brought a few strategically placed people and experiences into my path. Then a number of books I read seemed to shed a ray of light within my dark and discouraged thinking. As odd as it may seem, even Eponine's tender song was one piece of the puzzle.

I concluded that my bouts with depression couldn't be blamed on the losses of my childhood or the challenges of my adult life and ministry. My difficulties were not a matter of circumstance, but rather a problem with my thinking. It was not what someone had done or not done, but rather how I perceived what they had done. My mind had been programmed with incomplete and often false information from early in my childhood. Even my conversion to Christ and subsequent Christian growth had not corrected fully that faulty thinking.

This discovery was for me nothing short of revolutionary! It started me on a journey of learning how to renew my thinking and, as a result, change the direction of my life. I was amazed as I learned about how God designed our minds and what is to be the focus of our thought life. I came to realize that all of our spiritual progress and success as Christians begins in our thinking.

Man's Misconceptions

There are many misconceptions today about the connection between our thoughts and our lives. There are people who believe you can have spiritual growth without engaging your mind. At the same time, we are a more spiritual society today than we have ever been. Recent research statistics suggest that more people believe in God and heaven than at any other time in our history. Yet, very few people are finding their spiritual needs met. Why? Because, they are applying a "mind-less" spirituality to their life and discovering it doesn't satisfy.

Some people—including well-known writers and speakers—advocate that the answer is positive thinking. The power of positive thinking is offered as the solution to all that ails us. However, you can think positively about the wrong things and the results will not be ben-eficial. I can fall out of an airplane without a parachute and think positively all the way down; but, I'm still going to have a rude awakening when I reach terra firma.

God's Solution

Because man is a fallible being, any answers he comes up with on his own are always going to fall short. But there *is* one place we can go to for help: God, the one who created us and knows us best. God has revealed the solution to us in His Word, and it is this: If we want to experience true and lasting change in our lives, we need to use our minds as God intended. In Romans 12:2, the Lord tells us that a transformed life comes from a renewed mind.

In the pages ahead, we will discover together God's design for changing our minds. I'm sure you'll become excited as you see how much God's Word has to say about the way our thoughts can permanently change the way we think, feel, and live. Won't you join me, then, as we allow the power of God's Word to transform our lives?

Part 1

THE POTENTIAL FOR
RENEWING YOUR MIND

Changing the Way You Think and Live

The responsibility I had been given was both exciting and overwhelming: I had been asked to be the speaker at a high school Valentine's Day banquet. As a new seminary student, I was just beginning to learn the art of preaching, so my feeling of nervousness started long before the night of the banquet. What do you say to a group of teens on Valentine's Day, some with a date and others wishing they had one? Do you tell again the history of St. Valentine or talk about love? What would be the best way to capture their interest?

In the days that followed, I began to see the familiar signs of Valentine's Day in the stores. Of course, these included cards, flowers, and other similar gift options. I also noticed hearts everywhere—candy hearts, paper hearts, hearts on cards, and more. Then I came up with an idea: I decided to talk about the heart from a biblical perspective. Was I ever in for a surprise! I assumed I would be able to find a few Bible passages on the heart and on love, but what I found were over 800 references to the heart in Scripture! What also amazed me was how few of those references emphasized emotions.

The more I studied many of the references to the heart, the more my talk to the students changed from a discussion of love and emotions related to Valentine's Day to a challenge to recognize the heart as the center of a person's life and the key to his success.

The Heart of the Matter

The talk that I finally gave was, I hope, helpful to those who listened, but I'm sure I got much more out of the study than they did. For instance, when I came to the familiar passage in Proverbs 3:1-6, I gained a completely new perspective on the heart:

> My son, do not forget my teaching, but keep my commands in your heart, for they will prolong your life many years and bring you prosperity. Let love and faithfulness never leave you; bind them around your neck, write them on the tablet of your heart. Then you will win favor and a good name in the sight of God and man. Trust in the Lord with all your heart and lean not on your own understanding; in all your ways acknowledge him, and he will make your paths straight.

These verses teach us three vital truths: God's commandments are to be kept *in* our heart, we are to write love and faithfulness *on* the tablet of our heart (what a descriptive phrase that is),[1] and we are to trust in the Lord *with* all our heart.

Proverbs 4:23 also stood out in my study: "Above all else, guard your heart, for it is the wellspring of life." I had always assumed that when the Bible spoke of the heart, it described the amazing pump that beats in our chests more than 58,000 times every 24 hours, sending blood coursing through our veins. And I expected that the Bible would describe the heart as we might on Valentine's Day when we say to our significant other, "You have stolen my heart," or "I love you with all my heart."

What I discovered in my pursuit was that most of the time the heart was described neither as the seat of emotions nor a physical organ, but rather as the center of a person's life. The heart, for Solomon and the other writers of Scripture, is the command center where an individual thinks, reasons, decides, and feels.

With that description in mind, let's read Proverbs 4:23 again: "Above all else, guard your heart, for it is the wellspring of life." Now allow me to offer this paraphrase: "This is a most important subject so consider it carefully. Guard your heart, for it is the command center of your being where your thoughts form and your decisions are made. Out of this wellspring will come all the important issues of life."

Notice that the verse speaks of the heart as the wellspring of life. That led me to wonder: What produces the "water" that bubbles up from the wellspring? What determines the content and quality of the thoughts that originate there? Do we have any control over what comes out of our heart and bubbles up into our life? I believe as we find Scripture's answers to these questions, we'll find the results life-changing.

The Heart and Mind

The words, actions, and emotions that bubble out of your heart into your life are an effect, not a cause. The Old Testament prophet Jeremiah is very clear that a sinful heart produces sinful behavior when he says,

> The heart is deceitful above all things and beyond cure. Who can understand it? "I the LORD search the heart and examine the mind, to

reward a man according to his conduct, according to what his deeds deserve" (Jeremiah 17:9-10).

Jesus dealt with this same issue when He challenged the Jewish teachers of the law about their obsession with rules related to cleanliness and eating.[2] When His disciples asked about His rebuke, Jesus said,

> "Don't you see that nothing that enters a man from the outside can make him 'unclean'? For it doesn't go into his heart but into his stomach, and then out of his body." (In saying this, Jesus declared all foods "clean.") He went on: "What comes out of a man is what makes him 'unclean.' For from within, out of men's hearts, come evil thoughts, sexual immorality, theft, murder, adultery, greed, malice, deceit, lewdness, envy, slander, arrogance and folly. All these evils come from inside and make a man 'unclean'" (Mark 7:18-23).

According to the Bible, the heart and mind are linked, and they form the core of a person's being, as the writer of Proverbs so clearly states: "As a man thinks in his heart [mind] so is he" (Proverbs 23:7). In Scripture, the words *heart* and *mind* can be used interchangeably, just as in the proverb we just quoted. Many times they are discussed in the same verse, as in Philippians 4:7, where Paul says, "The peace of God, which transcends all understanding, will guard your hearts and your minds in Christ Jesus." In any case, when we discuss either the heart or mind in the coming pages, we are using them synonymously—and for the purposes of this book, we will place the emphasis on the mind.

Sowing and Reaping

John Stott, in his book *Your Mind Matters,* made this excellent observation about the heart and mind as the center of our being:

> Self-control is primarily mind control. What we sow in our minds, we reap in our lives. Feed the Minds was a slogan for a campaign of Christian literature. It bore witness to the fact that men's minds need to be fed as much as their bodies. And the kind of food our minds devour will determine the kind of person we become.[3]

You are today the sum of all the thoughts you've had over the past months and years. It can also be said that you will become the product of the thoughts that fill your heart and mind in the hours and days ahead. Who would you like to become? What kind of person do you envision yourself being in the future?

Perhaps there are things in your life that you'd like to change. Is worry a problem for you today? How about lust or fear? Do you desire to see your worry replaced with peace, your lust with purity, and your fear with trust? Whatever your concern might be, the Bible says change is possible—it all begins with a renewed mind. I believe I can demonstrate from Scripture that your mind is the key to your success in the problem areas we just mentioned, plus many more.

The Key to Change

Some years ago as I struggled with my own bouts of discouragement, I searched through self-help and psychological books in hopes of discovering an answer, but I found none. Then one day as I was reading Romans chapter 12, I suddenly understood for the first time a verse I had memorized years before: "Do not conform any longer to the pattern of this world, but be *transformed by the renewing of your mind"* (Romans 12:2).

It was as if a light turned on in my mind. That was my problem! I wanted to be transformed, but I didn't have the slightest idea of how transformation took place. The words "by the renewing of your mind" seemed to jump from the page. If I wanted to be transformed, then I needed to *renew my mind*. That led me to my next question, which is the focus of this book: How does a person renew his mind? Together, we're going to see that *a mind renewed is a life transformed*.

The Prerequisites for Change

Where do we begin in this mind-renewal process? I believe it's helpful for us to begin by looking at a description of transformation that's found in 2 Corinthians 3:18. It reads, "We all, with unveiled face beholding as in a mirror the glory of the Lord, are being transformed into the same image from glory to glory, just as from the Lord, the Spirit" (NASB).

The Decision

The first truth is that *transformation is only possible for believers*. A few verses before 2 Corinthians 3:18, we are told that the Israelites who followed Moses through the wilderness had "minds [that] were made dull, for to this day the same veil remains when the old covenant is read. It has not been removed, because only in Christ is it taken away" (2 Corinthians 3:14). The same veil is spoken of in the very next chapter, where Paul says, "Even if our gospel is veiled, it is veiled to those who are perishing. The god of this age [Satan] has blinded the minds of unbelievers, so that they cannot see the light of the gospel of the glory of Christ, who is the image of

God" (2 Corinthians 4:3-4). But this condition need not be permanent, for "whenever anyone turns to the Lord, the veil is taken away" (2 Corinthians 3:16).

The veil that covers the mind and limits the understanding is removed only when a person turns to Christ as Savior and Lord. It is important for us not to rush past this point. The kind of transformation that's described in the Bible is *not possible* until a person has trusted Christ as Savior and has had the veil removed.[4]

While I was a seminary student and a youth pastor in a local church, a young woman came to me with a problem. She had fallen in love with a man who was very pleasant but was not a believer in Christ. She asked if I would talk with him. My wife and I invited them to dinner and when we had finished, I invited him to go out for a walk. While my wife and the young woman prayed, I tried to share the good news of Jesus with him. He seemed interested, but when I asked, "Is there any reason you couldn't receive Jesus right now?" He said, "Yes." At first I thought this meant he was resistant and he didn't want to continue. Unsure of what to say next, I asked what his reason was for not accepting Jesus. His response surprised me; he said he didn't understand baptism. Relieved that he still appeared to be interested, I explained that baptism is a symbol of the change that takes place when a person receives Jesus Christ as Savior. After I clarified that baptism was not necessary for salvation but that it was an act of obedience that follows salvation, I asked him again, "Is there any reason now that you couldn't receive Jesus?" He answered, "No." After a moment of nervous silence, I explained the salvation message again, and he prayed to receive Jesus. The veil had been removed! His eyes were now open, and in the years that have followed he has continued to grow and mature.

The Guidebook

The second truth is that *transformation is Word-centered.* Once the veil is removed through receiving Christ, then God's Word becomes the guide for a changed life. Second Corinthians 3:18 says, "We all, with unveiled face beholding as in a mirror . . . are being transformed" (NASB). The "mirror" in which we behold "the glory of the Lord" is God's Word. In 1 Corinthians 13:12, we read, "Now we see but a poor reflection as in a mirror; then [when we get to heaven] we shall see face to face." We don't see God face to face now because we are human and earthbound, but we *can* see His reflected glory in the mirror, His Word.

The apostle James also refers to God's Word as a mirror when he says, "Do not merely listen to the word, and so deceive yourselves. Do what it says. Anyone who listens to the word but does not do what it says is like a man who looks at his face in a mirror and, after looking at himself, goes away and immediately forgets what he looks like" (James 1:22-24). Note carefully what James wrote next: "But the man who looks intently into the perfect law that gives freedom, and continues to do this, not forgetting what he has heard, but doing it—he will be blessed in what he does" (James 1:25).

What if you were to do a quick survey of your schedule right now? What might it reveal? Could it be that little time is being spent reading God's transforming Word in comparison with watching television or occupying yourself with other pursuits?

The Focus

The third principle mentioned in 2 Corinthians 3:18 is that *transformation is Christ-centered.* Going back to our key verse, we read that we are "beholding as in a

mirror the glory of the Lord, [and] are being transformed into the same image" (NASB). How do we become
Christlike? How are we formed into His image? By mod-
eling our lives after the life of Jesus. And how can we
best do that? By looking at His life as it is portrayed in
God's Word, the Bible. When we look in the mirror of
God's Word, our central focus will be the glory of Jesus
Christ as He lives His life before us and reveals His principles for living. Transformation isn't self-centered, as
many self-help programs tell us. Rather, it is Christ-centered.

The apostle John describes the end product that will
emerge when Christ finally returns for us: "Dear friends,
now we are children of God, and what we will be has not
yet been made known. But we know that when he
appears, we shall be like him, for we shall see him as he
is" (1 John 3:2).

The more we see of Jesus, the more we will be like
Him, and the beginnings of that transformation are
already available for those who discover Him in God's
Word. The reason so many believers seem to progress
so slowly toward Christlikeness is explained in a
warning that the apostle Paul gives the Corinthians: "I
am afraid," he says, "that just as Eve was deceived by
the serpent's cunning, your minds may somehow be led
astray from your sincere and pure devotion to Christ"
(2 Corinthians 11:3). *Christ* must be the focus of our
devotion if we desire transformation.

The Process

The fourth truth is that *transformation is a process.*
Now I'm sure most of us would like instantaneous transformation! We would like God to miraculously remove
all the faults, habits, and thought patterns that we detest
and replace them immediately with right thinking and

acting. But, Paul made it very clear in 2 Corinthians 3:18 that we "*are being* transformed." The phrase "are being," in the original Greek text, is a present participle which indicates that our transformation is continually going on in the present. Our growth proceeds hour by hour and day by day as a process. Many of us may wish we could be like the popular mythical character Superman, who is "able to leap tall buildings in a single bound." However, God describes the process of transformation as taking place one step at a time. We are to "keep in step with the Spirit" (Galatians 5:25) moment by moment, and as we do, He will transform us "from glory to glory" (2 Corinthians 3:18 NASB). Another way to say that is "from glory to ever increasing glory," or "glory layered upon glory." In other words, the transformation of our lives is an exciting process of dynamic growth that continues until we are in the presence of Christ in all His glory!

The Strength

There is one final truth that's foundational to our growth: *Transformation is a work of the Spirit.* The end of 2 Corinthians 3:18 reads, "Just as from the Lord, the Spirit," or, as the NIV reads, "With ever-increasing glory which comes from the Lord, who is the Spirit."

This final element is vital if we want to complete the mosaic of transformation. Our human efforts will never be sufficient to change us. That is where all the "secrets of success" concocted by men fall short. They ignore the Source of Strength for change. The resources for our transformation are not of human origin. Oh yes, we are to apply the Scripture's principles with our minds and wills, but to do so even in our best energies will only guarantee failure. It is the Holy Spirit who empowers us to accomplish the transforming process. As we keep in step with the Spirit, He guides us through the process of being transformed by the renewing of our minds.

Are You Ready?

I want to ask you five very important questions that will help you to personalize what we've just learned:

1. *Is your face unveiled?*

   Have you received Jesus Christ as your Savior and Lord? The changed life that you seek is possible only for a person who has received Christ and has had the blinders removed.

2. *Are you willing, as a believer, to look regularly into the mirror of God's Word?*

   The discipline of faithfully reading and studying God's Word is at times difficult. You may discover truths about God and yourself that make you uncomfortable or perhaps are even painful.[5] The Word of God, however, is the only truly effective guidebook for bringing about transformation. Pursuing God's Word may require setting aside some other pursuits, turning off the TV, or changing your busy schedule to make time for discovering God's truths. Are you willing?

3. *Are you willing to be Christ-centered?*

   Being Christ-centered assumes that you don't have something else at the center of your life. It may mean dethroning sports, shopping, self, or even placing a very important person in your life in a secondary position to Christ.

   This pure devotion to Christ is described so well in a wonderful little booklet written years ago by

Robert Boyd Munger called *My Heart—Christ's Home*.[6] In a few pages, Munger paints a picture of a person's heart as a house. Each room is descriptive of one area of our lives. For example, the recreation room is where we have our hobbies and recreational activities. The study is where the mind is fed through books, magazines, tapes, and videos. Located in the dining room are the appetites and desires of our lives. The living room, however, is a quiet place where Christ wants to meet us regularly for fellowship and communion.

Ultimately, the point of Munger's booklet is that Christ wants to possess all of the home. He wants to be the Lord of every area of our lives, thus making us completely Christ-centered.

4. *Will you accept that the transformation of your life is a process?*

Or, to say it another way, will you reject the so-called "quick fixes" and commit yourself to the biblical process of change? This may mean altering lifelong habits and adjusting comfortable patterns that run counter to the process. It may at times seem frustratingly slow. Will you say yes anyway?

5. *Finally, will you let God's Holy Spirit lead you?*

Are you willing to say. "I can't do this, Lord; I've tried before. But I will let You lead and give me the strength to change." Transformation is a spiritual process that cannot be accomplished by human efforts alone. As you respond to God's Word, guided by the Holy Spirit, God will transform you toward greater Christlikeness.

Where Do We Go from Here?

In the following chapters, we will see how a changed mind leads to a changed life. We'll also look at how this renewing is accomplished and discover just a few of the many benefits and blessings of having a renewed mind.

It *is* possible for you to renew your mind and see your life transformed! If that weren't possible, then Paul would not tell us, "Do not conform any longer to the pattern of this world, but *be transformed by the renewing of your mind"* (Romans 12:2, emphasis added).

Would you like to see transformation take place in your life? Have you been struggling with negative and destructive thoughts? Are you bound by habits and addictions formed through years of sinful practice? Are there times when, with the apostle Paul, you cry out, "What a wretched man I am! Who will rescue me from this body of death?" (Romans 7:24).

The answer to your cry is found in the person of Christ and in the biblical process of transformation, which takes place through the renewing of your mind. Are you willing to take the first step?

Prayer

Father, I commit myself to this process of renewing my mind. Please demonstrate Your power and Your truth to me in this study. I pray that Your Spirit will work in my heart as my mind is renewed and my life transformed for Your glory. In Christ's name, amen.

Releasing the Captive

Your excitement mounts as the chairlift takes you to the top of the mountain. From there, you get an absolutely breathtaking view that extends for miles. You then test your skis, which by now feel almost like extensions of your legs. They glide so effortlessly across the newly fallen white powder snow. The air is crisp and fresh but surprisingly, it doesn't seem cold even with all the snow covering the mountainside and trees around you. Maybe it's the thrill of the moment that guards you against the chill. As you drop over the face of the head wall and rapidly gain speed, the only sounds are the wind whistling past your face and the skis slicing through the snow.

Suddenly, the computer screen before you flashes and jars you back to reality. The noise of the office around you assaults your ears as you return grudgingly to your responsibilities.

Have you ever daydreamed like that before? Your experience is not unusual. The same phenomenon takes place in offices and factories all over the world on Fridays—and sometimes earlier in the week! Workers are still laboring over their lathes or keyboards, but their minds are far away on a mountain slope or on a sandy beach. The plans for the weekend ahead have captured their minds.

At times we hear music or drama critics use the word *captivating* to describe a certain performer or play they are reviewing, saying that the audience was completely enthralled with the performance, which lifted their minds above the realities of life. The human mind is such that it can be taken captive and pirated away to a beautiful South Sea island of happiness or a dark, cold dungeon of despair.

There are many competitors vying for your conscious thoughts hour after hour. Some are as innocent as a daydream about a weekend ski trip. Others are so powerful that they can plunge you into hours or even days of anxiety or depression. Certainly God wants to capture and direct your thoughts in ways that will benefit you and please Him, but He is not alone in this desire to control your thinking. There is another who would like to capture your mind as well.

The Battle for Our Minds

According to Scripture, one of those who strives to take your thoughts captive is Satan, who "prowls around like a roaring lion looking for someone to devour" (1 Peter 5:8). There is a constant battle between God and Satan for our minds. I'm sure you've had times when you've attempted to read God's Word and found yourself constantly distracted—to the point that you came away from your study with little recollection of what you had read. Satan does not want you to absorb God's Word in general, nor does he want you to learn about renewing your mind. He knows you have the privilege of choosing what you will think about, and as often as he can, he will encourage you to dwell on thoughts other than those which please God.

Incessantly, distracting thoughts enter our minds. In response, we follow these detours down new routes and are soon vacationing in another thought world, completely detached from our original points of departure. These unscheduled "vacations" may last a few moments or even several hours!

However, such distractions are usually much more than simple detours. We are actually talking about a war. There is a battle going on for our minds, and they are often taken captive. We need to learn how to rescue them. We can know victory only when we allow our minds to be captivated with thoughts from God rather than from Satan.

The Bible clearly affirms that we're engaged in a war for our thoughts. In Ephesians 6:12 we read that "our struggle is not against flesh and blood, but against the rulers, against the authorities, against the powers of this dark world and against the spiritual forces of evil in the heavenly realms." In that same passage, we are told God has supplied armor for us to wear in the battle, including the helmet of salvation to protect the mind. The battle is between the spiritual forces of good and evil; the apostle Paul states, "I see another law at work in the members of my body, waging war against the law of my mind and making me a prisoner of the law of sin at work within my members" (Romans 7:23). A parallel passage is found in James 4:1: "What causes fights and quarrels among you? Don't they come from your desires that battle within you?" The desires of your life, good and bad, wage war on the battlefield of your mind.

Most likely this conflict has been evident recently in your own life. In the last few days, how often did thoughts enter your mind which you knew were displeasing to God? Perhaps you put up a struggle, not wanting to give in. If you did give in, what actions resulted from these improper thoughts? Too often a mind taken hostage produces undesirable conduct. Any failure in your life first begins in your mind. This is always the order and shows us how vital it is for us to know how to *renew* our minds.

The enemy is real. For that reason, the Bible has a great deal to say about Satan. God wants us to understand how the enemy functions and what tactics he uses in our lives. God also wants us to know that we have resources available to fight in this conflict. In fact, Christians already possess these weapons, but often fail to use them. Why? Because many do not understand God's instructions for their use and thus have not succeeded in defeating the enemy in their lives.

Satan, at one point in history, was an exalted angel in the heavens. He was a powerful, brilliant being created by God. He was cast from heaven because of his insurrection against God, and now is our deadly enemy.[1] We dare not underestimate his power and influence. Our human resources literally disintegrate in the face of satanic assaults. We *must* understand this truth!

The Weapons God Provides

In 2 Corinthians 10:3-4, Paul says, "Though we live in the world, we do not wage war as the world does. The weapons we fight with are not the weapons of the world. On the contrary, they have divine power to demolish strongholds." Man's weapons cannot be used in this conflict. Our attempts to use human reasoning and logic or to apply even our best efforts in our own strength will be futile. But we do have resources available to us for fighting the battle. Those resources are from God and are divinely powerful. In the verse above, the Greek word for "power" is the root from which we get our English word *dynamite*. Divine dynamite is available for you to fight the war! That's why we are told, "Be strong in the Lord and in his mighty power" (Ephesians 6:10). According to Scripture, we have basically three spiritual resources—three weapons available for us to use in the battle for control of our minds. The first is the Word of God. In Ephesians 6:13-17, we are told to put on the whole armor of God. One piece of that armor is "the sword of the Spirit, which is the word of God." This sword gives us not merely *defensive protection*, but *offensive strength* as well. "I believe that," you whisper in your heart. Do you? Then be honest with yourself: How much time in the last week did you spend nourishing and building yourself in God's Word? You can be sure that Satan worked energetically to capture your thoughts and make them his hostage. How diligent were you in using God's Word to defend yourself against your enemy?

The second resource at our disposal is the powerful Holy Spirit of God. The same verse that describes our sword tells us it is supplied by the Spirit. The Holy Spirit works in cooperation with us to wield the sword of God's Word in order to overcome Satan's attacks on our minds. The Spirit is able to supply divinely powerful resources at the very moment of our need. Have you allowed Him to take control of your mind and your actions to give you victory in areas that might otherwise have been lost in battle?

The third powerful resource is prayer. Ephesians 6:18 tells us to put on the armor, "and pray in the Spirit on all occasions with all kinds of prayers and requests. With this in mind, be alert and always keep on praying for all the saints."

Many years ago, E.M. Bounds, a godly man of prayer, wrote a book entitled *The Weapon of Prayer*. Both the title and contents emphasize the power of prayer in winning the battle with sin and Satan. Bounds says,

> Nothing is more important to God than prayer in dealing with mankind. But it is likewise all-important to man to pray. Failure to pray is failure along the whole line of life. It is failure of duty, service, and spiritual progress. God must help man by prayer. He who does not pray, therefore, robs himself of God's help and places God where He cannot help man.[2]

It is prayer that hooks all of our armor together and prevents the evil one from finding areas of weakness in our defenses. Through prayer, we can literally enter into the throne room of God with all of our needs in the midst of trial and temptation.[3]

The Word of God, the Spirit of God, and prayer are divinely powerful weapons available to us for demolishing the strategies of Satan. Human resources will fail, but God's weapons will never let us down in the battle.

Satan's Strategy

What is Satan's strategy? What is he trying to accomplish in our minds? We dare not remain ignorant of his schemes.[4] We need to know what Satan is doing in order to be able to defend ourselves.

Building Strongholds

First, Satan is setting up strongholds in our minds against the knowledge of God.[5] He does not want people to know God at all. However, if you already believe in Jesus as your Savior, then Satan changes his tactic: He tries to stop you from gaining more knowledge of God. The more you know God, both in your mind and in your daily walk with Him, the less likely you will be to succumb to satanic influence and thus remain useable to God. Second Peter 1:3 states that everything we will ever need for life and godliness is available to us through a full knowledge of God. One of Satan's chief designs, then, is to keep us from that knowledge. If he can build a wall or stronghold around our thinking, he can then keep out the true knowledge of God.

How does Satan execute this plan? He is the arch-deceiver, chief of all liars.[6] For that reason, he works subtly. Seldom does he immediately introduce a gross and immoral thought to our minds, for he knows we would recognize its origin and most likely resist it. Rather, he sets up the stronghold one stone at a time.

An excellent illustration is the temptation of Eve. In Genesis 3:1, Satan raised a question in Eve's mind as to God's fairness in forbidding her to eat the fruit from the Tree of the Knowledge of Good and Evil. First, Satan took the liberty of misquoting God's words. Then he engaged Eve in further conversation, which she allowed, thereby placing herself on the defensive (verses 2-3). Trying to respond to Satan, Eve misquoted God's words and watered them down into generalities. Now Satan had Eve where he wanted her. Then in verse 4, he appealed to her pride. Speaking with a tone of authority, he directly contradicted God and tried to remove Eve's fear of God. Bible teacher Dr. Earl Radmacher says, "The devil's top strategy in the battle for your mind is to lower your concept of God. He diminished Eve's concept of God, and the consequences speak for themselves."[7] Satan then convinced Eve to try something she had not experienced before which would supposedly "liberate" her. By the time Satan was finished, he had appealed to Eve's eyes, her intellect, and her pride—a pattern clearly described for us in 1 John 2:15-17.

Look back on your own experiences. Is that the same way Satan approached you? Most likely he placed one questionable thought in your mind. If you allowed that one thought to remain, then that opened the door for him to bring in another and another, one stone at a time, until his stronghold was built.

What kinds of strongholds does Satan erect? The stronghold of humanism is prevalent in most believers' minds today. Humanism is the philosophy that places man at the center of his world and ignores God. Television is one of the main venues through which humanistic ideas and attitudes are fed into our minds. People, with their perversions and worldly philosophies, speak to us in our living rooms who would never be welcomed into our homes if they knocked on the front door. Humanistic perspectives are also taught in school and university classrooms as well as through books, magazines, and newspapers. Satan's goal through all this is to gradually have you thinking the world's way.

Lust is another stronghold. Satan starts small. In a young boy's life, he may use pornography. Just one picture, just one thought. If the boy has not, by age 14 or 16, dealt with these temptations God's way, Satan will be well on his way to building a solid fortress that may entrap the young man for the rest of his life. When he is 60 years old, those same thoughts and evil imaginations will still haunt him.

Examples of other strongholds Satan establishes in our minds are those of anger and bitterness. A small seed begins to grow, perhaps against an individual or circumstance. Then it is watered and fed. Soon it springs out of your mind and into actions which defile everyone around you.[8] God's divinely powerful resources are needed desperately to tear down these fortresses so that your mind can be renewed, and consequently, your life can be lived righteously to the glory of God.

Raising Up Speculations

Along with establishing strongholds, Satan's strategy includes building speculations within us.[9] In Scripture, the idea of speculation refers to human reasoning as opposed to God's wisdom. In 1 Corinthians 3:18-20, the apostle Paul wrote,

> Let no man deceive himself. If any man among you thinks that he is wise in this age, let him become foolish that he may become wise. For the wisdom of this world is foolishness before God. For it is written, "He is the one who catches the wise in their craftiness"; and again, "The Lord knows the reasonings of the wise, that they are useless" (NASB).

Notice Paul says that faulty thinking can lead us to deceive ourselves. We can literally deceive ourselves into believing that something which God calls unwise is really quite clever. God's wisdom appears foolish to human reasoning, but His wisdom is, in fact, the basis for successful living now and ultimate security in eternity. Worldly wisdom often appears very brilliant when it is actually utter foolishness!

The vast majority of believers today, unfortunately, use human reasoning to make the decisions of their lives. They allow the world's wisdom to dictate whom they should marry—someone who is physically attractive and yet spiritually incompatible. They raise their children with the help of the late Dr. Spock rather than the apostle Paul. Their decisions concerning a move, a major purchase, or how to live life in general may be made with no reference whatsoever to God's Word. The result is often great frustration because the world's wisdom results in pain and confusion.[10]

Lofty Things

According to 2 Corinthians 10:5 NASB, Satan has also been raising "every lofty thing" within our minds to keep us from a true knowledge of God. Pride is a good example. Human arrogance hates to admit to dependence upon anyone or anything—least of all, the Almighty God. A family is destroyed because a husband treats his wife and children with selfish disdain. A church is divided because the leaders are concerned for their own personal agendas and Satan has a heyday with people's self-centered, independent spirits. He is always encouraging people to do what is best for number one. It doesn't help that the media is constantly bombarding our minds with this message.

Another lofty thought Satan raises up in our minds is disobedience to God's Word. For example, let's say there is a person at your workplace who seems to enjoy irritating others. She has made your life difficult time after time and today, you finally blew up and told her off. At the time, you felt rather good about it, but on the way home, you remembered the verse that says, " 'In your anger do not sin': Do not let the sun go down while you are still angry" (Ephesians 4:26). You struggle within yourself all evening. One part of you says, "Call her and apologize," but the other part says, "She ought to apologize, not me, for she is the problem!" What do you do? Possibly you go to bed angry and try to justify your actions. Within a day or two, you have almost forgotten the incident. How quickly we can rationalize our sin of responding incorrectly to one of life's many situations! One stone at a time, Satan continues on with his strategies to control our minds.

Winning the War

I thank God that He not only makes us aware such a war exists but He also gives us His strategy for winning.

In 2 Corinthians 10:5, Paul wrote, "We are taking every thought captive to the obedience of Christ" (NASB). Victory is ours if we capture every thought for Christ.

What does Paul mean when he says "every thought"? Every thought that enters your mind is either God's thought or it is from another source. No thought is neutral. When a thought enters our minds, we need to examine it to determine its origin. "That," you might say, "is a lot of work!" Yes, but no one ever said war was easy. A soldier gives up most of the comforts of life and even places himself in jeopardy in order to reach his objective. An athlete spends years preparing herself for the Olympics, always placing her goals above her personal interests. Why should we expect to reach an objective as important as the transformation of our lives without doing battle at times?[11] Let's check those thoughts of anger, lust, pride, selfishness, fear, and doubt. Should we continue to dwell on those thoughts or dismiss them? Many of our thoughts will come directly from God and dwelling upon them will prove beneficial.[12] But often we let Satan's worldly thoughts go unrecognized. They are not dealt with immediately and as a result, our minds end up being taken captive.

It is reported that Martin Luther once said, "You can't keep the birds from flying over your head, but you can keep them from nesting in your hair." You can't decide what thought will come or what stimulus will be given you, but you can take an appropriate action in dealing with the thought when it arises.

How do we capture our thoughts and bring them into obedience? The next chapter will give you a specific, practical method for doing just that. However, don't go on without a brief review of what we have been saying.

We're in a war. Don't be lulled to sleep by the soothing but deceptive voices of society that say, "Don't be an alarmist, things aren't that bad. It's okay to be a Christian and still entertain thoughts that are contrary to the Bible. After all, that's just being broadminded." Don't even welcome any such thoughts for a moment!

Our enemy is exceedingly deceptive as well as powerful. It is important to not only recognize that we are in a war, but also to discover and depend upon the divinely powerful weapons at our disposal. Learn to use these weapons. Become accustomed to consciously carrying them with you hour after hour. Make God's Word a part of your daily armor while the Holy Spirit is your constant companion. And don't forget to "pray continually" (1 Thessalonians 5:17).

Fill your mind with God's thoughts and pray that the Holy Spirit will enlighten you whenever one of Satan's strategies is being used against you. When the Spirit shows you that an inappropriate thought has entered your mind, capture it and, with God's strength, bring it into obedience to Christ.

Is it your desire to see your mind renewed and your life transformed? Then begin right now with winning the war for your mind. And how can we do that? Read on.

Prayer

Help me, Father, to recognize how much of the world gets into me. Please give me the discipline necessary to fill my mind with Your thoughts from Scripture. Help me to take every thought captive and to check its source. Please, by Your Spirit, give me the help to commit myself in a greater way to having my mind transformed by Your powerful Word. In Jesus' name, amen.

Recapturing Your Thoughts

Neat Story

The water sparkled as the sun reflected off the waves that followed one another down the lake. The comfortably warm temperature, combined with a stunningly blue sky and a gentle but steady breeze, made it a perfect day for a novice sailor. Although my wife and I had both grown up in homes by Lake Minnetonka outside of Minneapolis and loved water sports, we had never tried sailing.

A few weeks earlier, we had purchased a small two-passenger sailboat that more closely resembled a surf-board with a sail than it did a masted schooner. However, to us it was a thing of beauty and grace. Our hearts raced with anticipation as we tightened our life vests, raised the sail for the first time, and prepared to push off to conquer the wind and waves.

Because the boat was small and we were accustomed to being on the water, it didn't seem important to us at that time to ask anyone for instructions in the art and science of sailing. After all, one only needs water, wind, a sail, and rudder as well as a smooth hull to ride the dancing waves—or so we thought.

My first mistake was made several hours before we launched out into the water. I had carefully waxed the boat, thinking the slippery surface would enhance the ride and increase the speed. In my zeal, I polished not only the bottom, but the deck as well. The moment the first wave washed over the boat, the deck became so slick that both of us slid helplessly off into the water. After a few moments of frantic swimming to reach the boat, we attempted with no success to climb back aboard. Finally, realizing the hopelessness of this endeavor, we swam to shore with the boat in tow and spent the next half hour applying strips of tape to the deck with the hope that they would provide enough traction for us to stay on board.

As you might guess, all of this uninvited frustration, as well as the unplanned exercise, gave me a strong desire to take a brief nap. My wife protested, but I told her I would be a far more effective captain if I rested my tired mind and body for a few minutes.

While I slept peacefully, the mutiny began. My wife persuaded a friend to join her and they quietly pushed the boat away from shore, raised the sail, and slipped out into the bay. They turned with the wind and, with the warm sun beating down upon them, began to sail with reckless abandon.

Their mutinous behavior was only made worse by the fact that they completely ignored the wise directive (drawn from my vast store of sailing knowledge) I had given them. Before I took my nap, I warned them never to sail downwind until they knew how to make their way back upwind.

The consequences of their actions were soon upon them when they reached the end of the lake and discovered that sailing against the wind was beyond their best efforts. For the next hour or so, they sat helplessly grounded on the sand while I slept blissfully. My tranquil state came to an end when I awoke and found my wife and our friend missing at sea, sailboat and all. After a few moments of panic, I scanned the shoreline and saw the brightly colored sail rocking on the beach a mile or so downwind.

I would love to tell you that I rushed to their rescue and taught my wife a much-needed lesson as I sailed masterfully upwind returning her safely to the point of departure. However, I must admit that my skills were not sufficient to move us even a hundred yards into the wind. We ended up being towed home behind a scruffy little motor-powered fishing boat with our heads hanging as the sail fluttered in the wind. All the way back, I thought of the wording for a classified ad I was going to place in the newspaper to sell our little sailboat.

The embarrassing problems we experienced on our maiden voyage were not as formidable as we might have thought. What we needed was some basic training in sailing skills. We did not understand how to use the wind rather than fight it. We had not yet learned how to set the sails to capture the wind and propel the boat to our chosen destination. Without this basic knowledge, we were unable to achieve the desired results with our boat.

Many of us are faced with a very similar problem when we seek to use our minds in a beneficial manner. Did you know that our thoughts are extremely important and they ultimately determine our actions and emotions? It's our thoughts that determine whether we'll respond to a circumstance with fear or courage, with worry or calm assurance. The circumstance doesn't determine how we will respond, our mindset does!

Setting Your Mind

The concept of "setting your mind" is quite common in the Scriptures. For example, in Colossians 3:1-2 Paul says,

> If then you have been raised up with Christ, keep seeking the things above, where Christ is, seated at the right hand of God. Set your mind on the things above, not on the things that are on earth (NASB).

Paul refers to the same truth again elsewhere:

> Those who are according to the flesh set their minds on the things of the flesh, but those who are according to the Spirit, the things of the Spirit (Romans 8:5 NASB).

> Finally, brethren, whatever is true, whatever is honorable, whatever is right, whatever is pure, whatever is lovely, whatever is of good repute, if there is any excellence and if anything worthy of praise, let your mind dwell on these things (Philippians 4:8 NASB).

Each of these sections of God's Word reveals a powerful insight for our mental, spiritual, and emotional well-being. Just as a sailboat is dependent not only upon the wind but also on the set of the sails, so does the set of our mind determine the course of our life.

Bringing Your Thoughts to Christ

In sailing, if you just allow a boat to seek its own course, it will undoubtedly go downwind and eventually end up on some shoreline as ours did that day. Many people live their lives that way. They allow the prevailing winds of circumstance to carry them along, moving them far from their desired destination.

However, in sailing, it *is* possible to go against the wind. The term used for this maneuver—which I learned after our experience—is *tacking*. One sets the sail so as to go into the wind at a 45-degree angle, then by reversing the angle a number of times, the boat can be made to zigzag and reach its safe harbor in spite of the wind's direction.

Just as the set of a boat sail determines the vessel's direction, so the set of the mind determines the ultimate destination of a person's life. What do you think about most often? What is your mindset? That determines where you go in life.

A biblical mindset will bring about the most favorable results, but oftentimes it's difficult to get our minds focused on what is most beneficial for us. After all, the winds of worldly thinking are very strong! They are beating on our small craft, sometimes brutally. So how can we get the sails set for the most beneficial port?

There is a method that has helped me greatly in recent years. It combines the concept of a biblical mindset with the idea of capturing our thoughts and bringing them into obedience to Christ. Just as the set of a boat's sail requires pulleys, ropes, and rigging, our mind is also aided by certain pieces of equipment. In 2 Corinthians, they are called "the weapons of our warfare" (10:4 NASB). They, like the ropes and pulleys, are very useful in helping us to have the mindset we want.

There are four words that remind me hour by hour of how to keep on course. They are *recognize*, *recapture*, *refuse* and *replace*. Let's look at each of them.

Recognize

Remember Paul said that we are to "take captive every thought to make it obedient to Christ."[1] In order to capture a thought, we must first recognize it for what it is. For example, you may be worried about your finances. You may be anxious because it's clear that your money is not going to last until the end of the month. Yet, Philippians 4:6 says, "Do not be anxious about anything." Read that verse again. It says, "Be anxious for nothing!"—not even your diminishing finances.

The moment you begin to worry, you must recognize the thought for what it is and respond appropriately. Anxiety is not an option. The winds of difficulty may be blowing against you, but you do not need to drift along with them.

Recognizing a thought for what it is assumes a number of things. First, you have the ability to discern whether the thought is worthy of your focus or not. One of God's weapons of warfare is borrowed from the arsenal right here, the weapon of God's Word. Revisit our sailing illustration with me for a moment. Suppose you know how to sail against the wind. But what if you are still on the lake when night falls? Suddenly, you realize you can't see the shore where you need to dock. You are sailing blind. That is when you must turn to your compass, which can help guide you over the dark waters to your desired destination. In your thought life, God's Word is the compass.

Scripture tells us that it is God's Holy Spirit who enlightens us and, in conjunction with the Scriptures, gives us the ability to recognize whether a thought is beneficial or detrimental to our well-being. The Holy Spirit's part in the sailing metaphor may be that of the rudder. The compass of God's Word signals the direction. The breath of prayer fills the sails, and the Spirit's rudder sets the course to the desired port.

Recapture

When you recognize a thought as an intruder that does not deserve to be welcomed, you want to capture that thought and bring it into obedience to Christ. Don't count on a detrimental thought to take care of itself. Remember, this is a war, and the enemy will plant thoughts in your mind in the hopes of deceiving you. Rather than allowing yourself to be held hostage by such thoughts, you must capture them and put them in their rightful place outside of your thought life.

Recapturing an errant thought is a conscious decision. You might say, "Here I am, worrying about my finances again. I know that is not beneficial to me nor is it acceptable to God. Therefore, I choose to capture that thought and deal with it God's way."

"But," you may ask, "what is God's way of bringing a thought into obedience to Christ?" The answer is found in the next two steps. After you have *recognized* and *recaptured* the thought, then you must *refuse* and *replace* it.

Refuse

You'll have many thoughts that you recognize as friends rather than enemies. If a thought is edifying, you'll want to welcome it. However, when you have recognized a thought as being sinful, such as the anxious thought we have discussed, you must refuse to allow that thought any further access to your mind.

The choice to refuse may be difficult. If the thought is worry, you may believe you have every right to worry. Or you may have become an inveterate worrier who has developed a tenacious habit of anxious thinking that is now your normal mindset. But, no matter how ingrained a thought may become, it must be refused. You can say, "Lord, I recognize this anxious thought as sin. I have recaptured it and desire to bring it into obedience to You. I refuse to allow it to remain in my thoughts any longer. Please strengthen me by Your Holy Spirit as I put this thought out of my mind."

We must not stop there, however. Refusing to think something can actually cause the thought to have more power in your mind. When you refuse to think some-thing, you are giving the thought even more attention. Is there a solution to this dilemma? Yes, there is: You must immediately replace the unacceptable thought with one that is appropriate.

Replace

Suppose I tell you not to think about a tasty piece of fruit you enjoy. Most likely, you'll find that the more you try not to think about the fruit, the more your mouth will water for it. However, if you choose not to think about fruit, but rather about your favorite dessert, then you've replaced one thought with another.

If worry is the offensive thought, then the replace-ment must be thoughts of God's faithfulness and care. When Jesus taught on anxiety related to our daily needs, He described how God cares for the simplest of His cre-ation, such as the birds and flowers. How much more will He care, then, for those of us who are His children? Jesus said, "Aren't you much more valuable than they?"[2]

We must choose to refuse a worrisome thought and replace it with God's promise. We must refuse destruc-tive thoughts and replace them with encouraging truths from God's Word.

Of course, the Bible is filled with truths that supply us with alternatives to faulty thinking. We can refuse thoughts of anger[3] and replace them with forgiveness.[4] Thoughts of fear can be replaced with thoughts of con-fidence in Christ.[5] We can refuse evil desires and in their place choose thoughts of righteousness and purity.[6]

Recognize, recapture, refuse, and *replace.* You'll find it well worthwhile to remember this pattern throughout each day. At first this may seem a repetitive and even ineffective exercise; but, if you continue consistently, soon you'll find that the offending thoughts you've had

are losing their power and your mindset is being repro-
grammed with truth.

Staying on Course in Strong Winds

There are many winds of destructive thinking blowing all around us, but they will not drive us off course if
we recognize them for what they are. These faulty ways
of thinking usually reveal that we have a *secular* mindset
rather than a *spiritual* one. Paul strongly encourages us
by saying, "Set your minds on things above, not on
earthly things."[7]

Related to that is the problem of having a *temporal*
rather than *eternal* mindset. You may remember 2 Corinthians 4:18, where we are told that we must "fix our eyes
not on what is seen, but on what is unseen. For what is
seen is temporary, but what is unseen is eternal."

There is also a danger of a *psychological* rather than
a *biblical* mindset. In our society, it has become almost
universally accepted that psychology has somehow
added new and necessary truth to what God has said in
His Word. The belief, it seems, is that God's Word is truth
but it is not all the truth, and that psychology can help
supplement the incomplete biblical information. The
Scriptures, however, say of themselves that *everything*
we need for life is found therein. Review with me again
Paul's words to Timothy:

> All Scripture is God-breathed and is useful for
> teaching, rebuking, correcting and training in
> righteousness, so that the man of God may be
> thoroughly equipped for every good work
> (2 Timothy 3:16-17).

A fourth faulty way of thinking is to have a *self-
centered* rather than a *Christ-centered* mindset. We find
this type of thinking exemplified among the "enemies of

the cross" described by Paul in Philippians 3:18-19, whose "god is their stomach, and their glory is in their shame. Their mind is on earthly things." By contrast, the true believer is a citizen of heaven who eagerly awaits the Savior, Jesus Christ.[8] The challenge for every Christian is found in Hebrews 3:1, which states, "Therefore, holy brothers, who share in the heavenly calling, *fix your thoughts on Jesus*, the apostle and high priest whom we confess" (emphasis added).

Setting the Sail

What is the set of your sail? Are you willing to take your thoughts captive and bring them into obedience to Christ? Will you determine your course not by the wind of the world, but by the compass of God's Word? If so, then the choice presented in the next chapter will help you to begin the process of renewing your mind and transforming your life!

Prayer

Dear Lord, help me to recognize my thoughts for what they are. Help me then to recapture them and bring them into obedience to You. May my mind be set on things above, where Christ is seated at Your right hand. Help me to make Your thoughts my thoughts as I begin this process of renewing my mind. In Jesus' name, amen.

4

Choices That Bring Change

Brother Lawrence, a seventeenth-century French-
man, entered a monastery with high expectations.
He wanted nothing more in his life than to know
God intimately. He anticipated that he would have the
privilege of spending hours on his knees in prayer and
meditation. His sole longing was to experience God's
presence, and what better place was there to do that but
a monastery?

When Brother Lawrence arrived at the monastery,
he was somewhat shocked when his superior told him
that his main task was to work in the kitchen washing
the pots and the pans. He thought that might be a temporary assignment; however, it wasn't. He continued to
work in the monastery kitchen for the remainder of his
life.

Initially, Brother Lawrence felt as if the kitchen work
was a hindrance to his desire to know God. But through
the years, he discovered a very important principle that
relates directly to our study about renewing our minds.
He learned that no matter where you are—even if you're
elbow-deep in greasy dishwater, it's possible to be in the
presence of God.

You may have read about Brother Lawrence in a little book that has been published and republished for hundreds of years, entitled, *The Practice of the Presence of God.*[1] As you read his wonderful story, you discover that this man, in the midst of what seemed to be very menial and frustrating circumstances, had his mind renewed and his life transformed. Although there were many challenges along the way, he never allowed them to deter him from his central goal. He made a choice that changed his whole life when he determined to practice the presence of God.

A Relevant Challenge

We could very easily appreciate the life of Brother Lawrence and yet feel that his experience has no application to us. After all, we live in a far more complex, fast-paced world. Brother Lawrence lived in seclusion behind the walls of an ancient monastery, where life moved at a different pace. The problems he faced were so simple in contrast with ours. Is it really possible for us to free ourselves of our modern world's countless distractions and obligations and ever hope to practice God's presence or experience a renewed mind?

The answer is clearly stated in a Scripture passage written many centuries before Brother Lawrence lived: "I urge you, brothers, in view of God's mercy, to offer your bodies as living sacrifices, holy and pleasing to God—this is your spiritual act of worship. Do not conform any longer to the pattern of this world, but be transformed by the renewing of your mind. Then you will be able to test and approve what God's will is—his good, pleasing and perfect will" (Romans 12:1-2).

That challenge was valid in the first century when Paul wrote it as God's inspired Word, and it is just as valid in our day. God never commands what He will not empower us to obey.

This passage, so central to our subject, is worthy of close consideration. In it, we will discover a very important truth for everyone who wishes to have a new mind and a transformed life.

Crossing the Bridge

Covered bridges have long been a favorite theme in paintings and photographs. There are parts of our country where tourists will plan their trips so they can visit covered bridges. My wife and I consider ourselves fortunate to live near several of these quaint, historic structures, which dot the countryside around our home. We enjoy discovering them and viewing the sometimes scenic rivers they cross.

With all of their nostalgic beauty, however, every covered bridge had one ultimate purpose: to help people get from one side of a river to the other. Those who live near covered bridges may get to the point where they hardly notice the aesthetic qualities of these bridges, but they would certainly be disturbed if a flood were to take out a bridge they needed to cross in order to get home.

Consider with me for a moment a bridge that may be standing in your path just ahead. It is the bridge of *consecration*. In a previous chapter, we discussed the need for regeneration when a person receives Christ and is given eternal life. It is not possible for a person to be renewed until he is first spiritually alive in Christ. In 1 Corinthians 2:14, we are told that "a natural man [one who does not have Christ as Savior] does not accept the things of the Spirit" (NASB). However, when a person has believed in the Lord Jesus Christ,[2] the all-important step of consecration is necessary. Webster defines *consecrate* as "to make or declare as sacred." From a biblical perspective, it means "to set apart or dedicate to the service of the Deity." For you to experience mind renewal, this bridge of consecration must be crossed by consciously setting yourself apart for God's service.

Crossing this bridge does not add to your salvation from sin, for that work is complete in Christ. What it does for you is provide new opportunities for spiritual growth.

Consecration or Conformity?

In light of God's great mercy toward us—in which He cleansed us from sin and gave us new life—we are called to "offer [our] bodies as living sacrifices, holy and pleasing to God."[3] Some people may feel it's enough that they have given their heart to Christ when they received Him as Savior, but what Paul is saying here goes beyond that. This is giving *all* of yourself to God as a sacrifice. You don't stop living, but you do stop living for yourself. Such consecration is a prerequisite for renewal.

What does that kind of consecration look like? Paul tells us in the next verse that a person who has given himself as a living sacrifice "[does] not conform any longer to the pattern of this world."

The word "conform" means to fashion yourself outwardly after a certain pattern. It comes from the Greek word *schema* which was often used to speak of a covering, a curtain, or a mask. For instance, you may have gone to a costume party dressed as a clown or a famous historical figure. You were still you, but your outer person was conformed to the character or image you represented.

In the early Greek plays and tragedies, the actors and actresses often held masks in front of their faces depicting happiness, anger, or sadness. The expressions on these masks were exaggerated so they could be seen by those in the upper seats of the theatre. A mask made an actor someone he was not; it changed him to fit his role.

That helps us to understand what it means to be conformed to the world: You outwardly blend in with your surroundings by wearing the mask that the world expects of you, but inwardly, the real you in Christ is hidden. Paul says, "Stop being conformed to the world!" Don't let the people around you set the agenda for your life, or as J.B. Phillips says, "pour you into its own mold."[4]

The Ways of the World

There are a number of ways we may find ourselves conforming to this world. First, we may conform to its *priorities*. In Colossians 3:5, Paul challenges us to put to death whatever belongs to our flesh, such as sexual immorality, impurity, lust, evil desires, and greed, which is idolatry. Daily we are pulled by the world to make these things our priorities. But Paul says, "You used to walk in these ways, in the life you once lived. But now you must rid yourselves of all such things as these" (verses 7-8).

The world also draws us into its *pursuits*. King Solomon listed many of these pursuits in the book of Ecclesiastes. He was so wealthy he could buy anything or anybody. He was so powerful, no one could limit his desires. But after trying everything there was to experience and enjoy in life, he summed up his experiment in doing and having it all as "meaningless, meaningless, everything is meaningless."[5]

We also are daily inundated with the *pressures* of the world. Peter exhorts us to respond to such pressure in this way: "Prepare your minds for action; be self-controlled; set your hope fully on the grace to be given you when Jesus Christ is revealed. As obedient children, do not conform to the evil desires you had when you lived in ignorance. But just as he who called you is holy, so be holy in all you do; for it is written: 'Be holy, because I am holy'" (1 Peter 1:13-16).

What pressures from the world are you experiencing? Are there influences at your job or school? Are your friends pressing you to conform? Could it be a constant drive to possess or to be somebody? If any of these worldly demands are causing you to conform to the world's ways, you will not be able to be transformed. The two are mutually exclusive.

Some Christians think that as long as they are conforming to the world's mold in just a few areas, they are not hurting themselves. They may say that I'm setting the standard too high and ask, "Can't a person be a little conformed and yet still be transformed?"

Well, in any athletic event, how far out of bounds is too far? Let's imagine we're in the final seconds of a big football game and victory depends on making a touchdown. The ball is hiked to the quarterback and he takes several steps back. The whole stadium is standing in nervous anticipation as he places a perfect pass into the waiting arms of the receiver, who miraculously eludes the grasp of two opponents as he runs toward the goal with every ounce of strength he has. His long strides take him within inches of the goal line . . . but then the tip of his right foot touches the sideline.

While the small misstep might not seem like much, it's enough for the referee to blow his whistle and call the receiver out-of-bounds. The crowd roars in disbelief as the outcome of the game has been decided by a barely noticeable infraction. The penalty didn't require that the player's whole body had to be out of bounds, but only the toe of his shoe.

When it comes to choosing between conformation or transformation, we're in the same dilemma. We will end up choosing one or the other. It's much like a glass of water that has only the tiniest speck of impurity in it—that speck is enough to make the whole glass impure.

The Transformation from God

What is transformation? While conformation is putting on a mask that makes an outward change, transformation is a complete change from the inside out. That's the concept conveyed by the English word *metamorphosis*, which is based on the word Paul used in the original Greek text of Romans 12:2. We use the word *metamorphosis* to describe the lowly caterpillar's change into a beautiful butterfly.

The same Greek word is used of Jesus in His transfiguration as recorded in Matthew 17. The deity of Christ, His glorious inner being, was briefly visible to the astonished eyes of Peter, James, and John.

It *is* possible for you to be transformed by the renewing of your mind! And ultimately, according to Romans 8:29, we will be conformed (the Greek word here speaks of metamorphosis) into the very image of Jesus Christ.

The Benefits of Transformation

Are there any benefits to being transformed? Absolutely, and a number of them are listed immediately in Romans chapter 12.

The first benefit is the ability to know God's will. Many Christians say they wish they could know what God desires for their life. In Romans 12:2, we read that when we are transformed by the renewing of our minds, then we will "be able to test and approve what God's will is—his good, pleasing and perfect will." A renewed mind is able to discern the will of God.

Second, you will be able to discover your true value is in Christ. A biblical and realistic self-esteem is possible for a believer who is being renewed. (We'll talk more about that in chapter 10.)

The third benefit that Paul describes is that each believer who is being transformed will discover his or her giftedness and place of significance in the body of Christ (Romans 12:4-8).

Better relations with other people—both believers and non-believers—is possible when you are being transformed (Romans 8:9-20); and, finally, even the pervasive sin of this world will no longer have a grip on you. You will no longer "be overcome by evil, but [will] overcome evil with good" (verse 21).

The message is clear. There are many benefits you will experience when you choose not to conform to the world, but rather to be transformed by the renewing of your mind.

Choices, Choices

Making a break from conformity to the world and setting a course toward renewed thinking and transformed living may be challenging at times. Some of our worldly habits may be deeply ingrained and difficult to throw aside. But the writer of Hebrews says this is exactly what we must do: "Let us throw off everything that hinders and the sin that so easily entangles, and let us run with perseverance the race marked out for us. Let us fix our eyes on Jesus, the author and perfecter of our faith, who for the joy set before him endured the cross, scorning its shame, and sat down at the right hand of the throne of God" (Hebrews 12:1-2).

Throwing off everything that hinders and then running the race suggests the need for repentance. *Repentance* is the biblical concept of turning away from our sin and turning toward Christ. It involves a change of mind that results in a change of direction.

Repentance and *remorse* are not the same thing, although many people today use those words interchangeably. *Remorse* is feeling sorry for sin only because one was caught and suffered the negative effects. *Repentance*, by contrast, recognizes the awfulness of sin and its disastrous results and then turns from it. Godly sorrow over sin leads to repentance and a new mindset that results in transformation. Worldly sorrow leads to remorse and a circular descent back into sin.[6]

To repent is to lay aside conformity to the world and fix your eyes on Jesus. Making that choice will mean a new and exciting change of mind and purpose for life.

All or Nothing

The bridge stands before you. Will you choose to cross over from being conformed to this world and begin the rewarding journey of mind renewal and life transformation?

Remember, you can't be both conformed and transformed. The decision here is radical and is described in the teachings of Jesus when He says, "If anyone would come after me, he must deny himself and take up his cross daily and follow me. For whoever wants to save his life will lose it, but whoever loses his life for me will save it" (Luke 9:23-24).

Becoming a living sacrifice is not 80 percent transformation and 20 percent conformation. It's not even 90 percent of one and 10 percent of the other. It's 100 percent consecration to God and His purposes in your life. The opportunities for spiritual growth that we'll explore in the upcoming chapters are dependent upon this choice. Let's cross the bridge to the other side . . . and begin a rewarding journey toward Christlike transformation.

Prayer

Father, I desire to make the choice to be no longer conformed to the world. I repent of my sin and self-centered desires. I give my body to You as a living sacrifice and commit myself, by Your strength, to begin the process of renewing my mind. I pray that You will show me how to be transformed into Christlikeness. In Jesus' name I pray, amen.

Part 2

The Process for Renewing Your Mind

Building on the Rock

Information

With the inevitable signs of death approaching, Sir Walter Scott lay on his bed, weakened in his struggle for survival. Lining the walls of his room were thousands of books. He was a very intelligent and literary man. Close friends and family stood quietly around the bed. Slowly, he turned his head and whispered, "Bring me the book."

"What book?" asked a startled relative as he glanced around at the shelves ladened with volumes of every kind.

"*The* book, the Bible," Sir Walter answered. "There is only one Book!"

Throughout the centuries, Christians have agreed that there is no book but *the* book to depend upon for all the important issues of life. From the very beginnings of the New Testament church, we are told that day after day, the believers "devoted themselves" to the study and application of God's truth (Acts 2:42). They made it the guidebook for their lives.

Is the Bible valued as greatly today by those who claim Christ as their Savior?

The Source of Information

Surveys are taken again and again by both the media and Christian organizations. The results seem to be consistent. Although the Bible is still at the top of the book sales charts, it is not widely read even by Christians. Recent polls suggest that just over 10 percent of Americans read the Bible on a daily basis. You may say, "That doesn't surprise me. After all, most of the people that were polled were not believers." However, the surveys that focus on those who claim to be born again are not much more encouraging. Only 18 percent of Christians say they open their Bibles on a daily basis, and some 23 percent of professing believers are on the other end of the spectrum, saying they never open the Bible at all!

Where then, do those who claim to know Christ get their information for living? What is their source for the answers to life's many questions?

Is the Bible really relevant for people living in an age like ours, or is it only an ancient relic?

A History Lesson

The church that I am privileged to serve in has a long and rich heritage. Seven of the pioneers who crossed the Oregon Trail gathered in a log cabin in the Southern Willamette Valley on July 1, 1852. They met to form the first church in the area and provide a place for worship, growth, and service. On that day so long ago, they opened a Bible that had traveled with them, read from it, and committed themselves to obeying its precepts.

Nearly 150 years later, First Baptist Church of Eugene is still founded upon God's inerrant and infallible Word.

Everything else has changed. There are no charter members left. Buildings have come and gone. The address has changed, as have the people. Programs are different and many of the ministries today bear only a faint resemblance to those before the Civil War.

But, God's Word hasn't changed at all, and we as a church believe exactly as we did on the day the church was founded. By the way, the Bible the pioneers used in forming the church is preserved in a glass case in our library for all to see. It reminds us of our roots, and describes for us our future as well.

Something That Lasts

In our constantly changing world, it is comforting to know that the truths and promises of God's Word will always remain the same. That's the very point which the prophet Isaiah made in Isaiah 40:6-8: "All men are like grass, and all their glory is like the flowers of the field. The grass withers and the flowers fall, because the breath of the LORD blows on them. Surely the people are grass. The grass withers and the flowers fall, but the word of our God stands forever."

Isaiah first describes the *permanence* of the Word. The flesh is temporary like the grass and flowers around us.

Some years ago, after my wife Lynda and I had moved to a new home in Oakland, California, a severe drought occurred. Some said it was the worst in 100 years. We were limited to using 35 gallons of water per day per person, so we were very careful not to waste this valuable resource. For example, I immediately ceased watering the lawn, and it wasn't long before our entire front yard looked like a concrete parking lot.

Our neighbor, however, kept on watering his yard because he wanted to keep the grass roots alive. When the rains finally returned, his yard was soon lush and green. But our lawn never recovered. "The grass withers and the flowers fall," Isaiah said. His words are somewhat uncomfortable, for he emphasized that all of us are just like grass. We, too, are temporary and will eventually wither and die.

Isaiah's contrast is equally clear. While the flesh is temporary like grass, on the other hand, the Word of God is permanent. It "stands forever."

Over the centuries, since God first revealed Himself and His purposes through the Bible, men and nations have come and gone. Philosophies have failed, intellects have turned to senility, religious systems have risen and fallen, but one thing has remained constant—God's Word!

Archeologists have unearthed long-forgotten civilizations, sometimes in an attempt to disprove the Bible, only to find dusty artifacts that reveal the truthfulness of God's eternal Word. Jesus confirmed the Bible's permanence when He said, "Heaven and earth will pass away, but my words will never pass away" (Mark 13:31).

Peter emphasized the same truth when he quoted from Isaiah 40 and then applied it by saying, "This is the word that was preached to you" (see 1 Peter 1:23-25). He was clarifying that the eternal Word includes the New Testament as well as the Old.

On a Mission

If God's Word is eternal, then certainly it has a mission to fulfill. Isaiah describes the *purpose* of God's Word when he quotes God, who says,

> "My thoughts are not your thoughts, neither are your way my ways," declares the Lord. "As the heavens are higher than the earth, so are my ways higher than your ways and my thoughts than your thoughts. As the rain and the snow

> come down from heaven, and do not return to it without watering the earth and making it bud and flourish, so that it yields seed for the sower and bread for the eater, so is my word that goes out from my mouth: It will not return to me empty, but will accomplish what I desire and achieve the purpose for which I sent it" (Isaiah 55:8-11).

God's Word never returns empty. It always accomplishes its purpose. God sends out His Word to save and it returns with a new believer. He sends forth His Word to strengthen and Christians are renewed and encouraged. God's Word challenges people and stimulates commitment and even repentance. It always accomplishes its mission.

"But," you may say, "some people who have read the Bible don't believe, and some Christians are not encouraged or changed when they read the Word." The problem, however, is not with the Word, but with the hearer.

Let me explain. A doctor may diagnose a rare disease and inform you that only one medication is available to effect a cure. He then gives you a prescription to fill. But unless you obey his orders, the disease will continue unabated. So if you don't get better, it's not the doctor or medicine that's at fault, but you, because you refused to heed the doctor's warning and take the medicine.

The same is true about the Bible. If we don't put it to work in our lives, then change cannot take place. If believed and obeyed, however, God's Word always fulfills its purpose and results in our profit. Do you remember Paul's words to Timothy? "All Scripture is God-breathed and is useful for teaching, rebuking, correcting and training in righteousness, so that the man of God may be thoroughly equipped for every good work" (2 Timothy 3:16-17).

God's Word is profitable for *every* area of our life and can make us complete. That suggests the Word must be given *priority* in our lives.

First Things First

Some misunderstandings may be cleared up if we recognize these three truths:

1. The Word was given not merely for discussion, but to be obeyed. We may sit in a group Bible study and discuss the prodigal son yet remain in a far country of sin eating the husks of a wasted life.[1] We may quote a verse on love yet continue to hold grudges and treat others with contempt. It's possible to piously read Philippians 2:3-4 about considering others more important than ourselves, and yet go on pursuing our own selfish purposes.

2. The Word was given not merely for satisfying our curiosity, but to be obeyed. We may know fact after fact of biblical knowledge and yet find our experience empty. Some individuals can spout a lot of information taken from the Bible, yet be a dry well when it comes to biblical living.

3. The Word was given not merely to elevate our emotions, but to be obeyed. A person may say, "I read the Bible because it makes me feel better." Another person goes from one church to another hoping to receive a new experience that will give him or her a spiritual high. The desire for emotional experiences without obedience is not new with our time. Listen to God's words to Ezekiel:

> As for you, son of man, your countrymen are talking together about you by the walls and at the doors of the houses, saying to each other,

"Come and hear the message that has come from the LORD." My people come to you, as they usually do, and sit before you to listen to your words, but they do not put them into practice. With their mouths they express devotion, but their hearts are greedy for unjust gain. Indeed, to them you are nothing more than one who sings love songs with a beautiful voice and plays an instrument well, for they hear your words but do not put them into practice. When all this comes true—and it surely will—then they will know that a prophet has been among them (Ezekiel 33:30-33).

The Word is meant to be a priority in every area of our lives. That's why James says, "Do not merely listen to the word, and so deceive yourselves. Do what it says" (James 1:22).

Everything Needed for Godliness

If we want to experience renewal in our lives, then we need to look to the information God provides in His Word. There are many sources of information, but only one is suitable for transformation.

When I was a child, I often saw my Dad come home from work and immediately go out in his boat to fish in the lake in front of our house. It was not unusual for him to bring back some fish, clean them and have Mom prepare them for supper. Dad's pattern was always the same: He would lay out some old newspapers on a table in the yard, clean the fish, and then wrap up the garbage and throw it away. For years, I thought we subscribed to the newspaper just for the purpose of wrapping up fish remnants. Now I know better, and in fact I myself read the paper every morning. It gives me the latest news information, but by the next day it's only good for wrapping up the garbage.

The Word of God, on the other hand, never gets old. It is just as pertinent today as it was when it was given to Moses, Isaiah, the apostle Paul, and the others who penned the Bible.

God's Word is the indispensable ingredient in renewing your mind and transforming your life. Everything you and I will ever need for life and godliness is found in a full knowledge of God.[2] God can be known fully only through His Word, the Bible.

Living in Constant Dependence

Dwight L. Moody, the evangelist, once explained that a man can no more take in a supply of grace for the future than he can eat enough food to last him for the next six months or take enough air into his lungs in one breath to sustain life for a week. We must draw upon God's boundless store of grace each and every day as we need it. We cannot just take a breath; we must keep on breathing. In the same way, we need God's Word to sustain us on a daily basis. No other source of information is capable of bringing about true renewal and transformation. The opinions and counsel we receive from the world around us constantly change and become outdated and irrelevant. What's more, those who are in a position to dispense their views and advice cannot even agree with each other. By contrast, John Murray wrote, "There is no situation in which we are placed, no demand that arises, for which Scripture as the deposit of the manifold wisdom of God is not adequate and sufficient."

Unleashing the Power of God's Word

How, then, do we reprogram our thinking with God's Word? There is a simple method of interacting with your Bible that I would like to describe briefly for you. More formally, this pattern of study is known as the inductive study method.

Observation

First, you need to find out what God says about the subject in which you are interested. That is *observation*. Let's say you have a problem with discouragement, and you decide to read a Bible passage that addresses this emotion. When you observe, you want to be careful not to read into the biblical text, but rather let Scripture simply speak for itself. After reading the passage two or three times, you can write down the basic facts, even if, at first glance, they seem unimportant. As you review this list of facts, you may find God's Word speaking to your heart.

You'll also want to look for other related passages. A Bible concordance is helpful here. Look for synonyms that relate to discouragement or perhaps its opposite, encouragement. By doing this you will establish a cross-reference of parallel passages on the subject at hand. Again, read each passage through several times. When you observe, you are simply trying to glean God's basic information on the topic.

Interpretation

The second step is *interpretation*. Observation is gathering together the information. Interpretation is discovering what it means. First, read the contents of the book or chapter where the verses are located. Try to discover who wrote it and why he did. Pray that the Holy

Spirit will give you understanding and that He will open your mind to the truth of the Word. Then, let Scripture explain Scripture. By using parallel references, it is amazing how God's Word sheds light on itself. After you have done that, if you need to, you can refer to Bible commentaries.

Application

The third step is *application*. What is God's Word asking me to do? How do the principles I've discovered fit into my life? It's when we take this final step that we can experience the life-changing power of God's Word.

You'll want to make use of the inductive method as you study God's Word daily so that you can get into a pattern of consistent growth. Ask the following questions each time you read a passage: What does it say (observation)? What does it mean (interpretation)? What is God's Word asking me to do (application)? As you carry out this process, God's Spirit will lead you into an exciting journey of discovering His truth and its meaning in your life.

You can begin the process right now. Perhaps, there is an area of your life in which you have been struggling. In response to the earlier chapters of this book, you have begun to take your thoughts captive by bringing them into obedience to Christ. But now you want to learn how to think differently about that issue and be renewed. Before you go on to the next step, focus for a while on God's principles in your area of concern. If it is worry, then use your concordance to find some Bible passages that relate to worry or anxiety. Over the next few days, using the inductive study method, read through each of the passages carefully and discover God's principles for overcoming your problem with worry. Allow His truth to saturate your mind and reorganize your thoughts.

As you do this, you will be reprogramming your thinking with God's eternal Word. You will be making use of the one resource God has specifically given you for renewing your mind—His information.

Read the Instructions

What is your reaction when you open a package and find, inside the box, a sheet of instructions with the words, "Some assembly required"? Shivers go up my spine whenever I read that phrase! I don't know about you, but for me, that phrase warns me that I'm about to face one or two of the worst hours of my life. Some assembly instructions are so complex or vague that I've wished I had spent a year or two in technical training for such tasks!

On a number of occasions when I've been faced with a project that requires assembly, I'll lay out all the pieces first and then try to assemble them without reading the instructions. I'll say to myself, "Surely I can figure this out." But, after some frustrating attempts to figure out how to get "A" to fit "B" before bolting them onto "C," I'll finally reach my exasperation point and look for the instructions. Not until I carefully follow the directions provided by the manufacturer will I know for certain that I'm doing the job correctly.

God, the Manufacturer who created us all, has written the instructions for life. His instruction manual is called the Bible. All of the directions for assembly and successful operation are included. Will you pick up the Book and begin to study its directions? If yes, then not only are there many hours of enjoyment and reward ahead for you, but also you will have taken the first step in the journey toward a renewed mind.

Prayer

> *Thank You, Father, for giving me Your infallible source of Information. Please, remind me to dig into Your Word daily so I can study Your principles for living. May the Holy Spirit continue to help me to respond in obedience to You. I pray in Jesus' name, amen.*

What's Gotten into You?

Memorization

When our son was only three years old, we began praying that God would allow him the privilege of attending a Christian school. Just as he started kindergarten, we were transferred to a new pastorate 2,000 miles away. Upon moving to our new home, we found we were near a superb Christian school, and needless to say, our hearts overflowed with thanksgiving to the Lord.

Often it was my lot to take my young son and three other little children to school. Seldom did I find their conversations very challenging to me. Almost every discussion included an in-depth report on the latest adventures of Ultra-Man. I never watched the program, but I knew every move he made. The children felt I needed to be informed.

One particular morning during this mundane routine, my lower nature began to assert itself. The inner conflict resulted in a grouchy attitude, and the meaningless chatter about Ultra-Man added fuel to the fire. In the middle of their discussion, however, one boy turned to his brother and said, "Hey, do you have your verse memorized?"

"Yeah!" answered the boy.

"Well, let's hear it."

So the boy quoted his verse for that week. My son chimed in with his, and soon every child was quoting verse after verse. Then I was really grouchy. I didn't even have a verse to quote! In years gone by, I had memorized many verses, but more recently, I had slipped into a mode of reading the Bible without retaining its contents.

After we arrived at the school and the kids filed out of the car, I sat quietly thinking about what had just happened. Those children had more verses fresh in their minds than I did! My emotions were mixed. Although I was happy the children were filling their minds with Scripture, I felt disappointed at myself as I realized how much I needed a fresh infusion of God's Word in my own heart and mind. God used that incident to prompt me to get back into the habit of memorizing Scripture.

RA17549482. Those letters and numbers undoubtedly mean nothing to you, but they changed three years of my life drastically. I was given them as a serial number when I joined the Army nearly 40 years ago. Today, many years later, I can still recite them just as quickly as I could when I was required to memorize them then. Everyone has the ability to remember.

Too often I hear fellow Christians bemoan the fact that they just can't seem to memorize Scripture. Yet, I know some who know the names of everyone in the lineup of a particular sports team. There are others who can recite numerous facts about their favorite TV or movie stars. And most of us can quote our social security, license plate, and telephone numbers without error.

When you really think about it, it is amazing what we can remember with a little effort!

For example, I can recall an incident that took place while I was in the ninth grade. During study hall, a totally nonproductive hour, a fellow nearby leaned over and said, "Do you want to hear a joke?" Knowing the guy was not a believer, I thought it best to say no. Against my will, however, he proceeded to tell his joke. It turned out to be a completely sacrilegious rendering of the Easter story.

To this day I can still remember what he told me, for he painted pictures in my mind as he spoke. Isn't it strange how easily a mind can retain unedifying thoughts yet we find it difficult to recall that which is excellent? The matter of memorization is definitely a part of mind renewal and is an essential tool for helping us in our continual struggles with sin.

God knows how important it is for us to have His Word in our minds. Through Moses, He told Israel:

> These commandments that I give you today are to be *upon your hearts*. Impress them on your children. Talk about them when you sit at home and when you walk along the road, when you lie down and when you get up. Tie them as symbols on your hands and bind them on your foreheads. Write them on the doorframes of your houses and on your gates (Deuteronomy 6:6-9, emphasis added).

Where does God want His Word? He wants it on the doorframes of your house because He wants your neighbors to know you are a Christian. Of course, to have His Word on your doorframe means more than simply placing a fish symbol or a cross in some visible place. Sometimes, I follow people with fish symbols or Christian bumper stickers on their cars and their driving is anything but a testimony of Christian grace. The public demonstration of our faith isn't a matter of external symbols or messages. Rather, the Lord asks us to live out our Christian faith before our neighbors, coworkers and even fellow freeway travelers. He also desires that His Word be on display in our attitudes and placed at the center of our family conversations. And most important of all, according to verse 6, He calls for His Word to be *upon our hearts*. That is memorization. You may read God's Word yet forget its truths because the mere act of reading does not necessarily enable us to remember. The best way to retain God's truth is through memorization.

A Life-changing Power

Is your Christian testimony on display in such a way that people have asked, "What has gotten into you?" Wouldn't it be exciting if members of your family or those at school or work asked you that question and gave you an opportunity to share about your faith? Then you could respond, "The Word of God has gotten into me!" When God's Word truly gets *into* you, your life will change, and that change will be evident to others.

There is tremendous potential for true change to take place when we internalize God's Word. This is confirmed in Psalm 119:9, where the psalmist asked, "How can a young man keep his way pure?" The answer? "By living according to your word." The phrase "according to" is extremely important. It means "in light of" or "in obedience to." How can my life be kept pure? By living in light of God's perfect and unchanging Word—not according to the advice, opinions, or insights of finite beings such as a psychologist, a scientist, or even a friend.

Jesus Himself affirmed this truth in John 15:3, where He declares that we are clean because of His Word. The word "clean" here in the original Greek text is *catharsis*, which has to do with purging or cleansing. When Scripture gets into our minds, it will sweep out the cobwebs, confusion, and worldly debris. God's Word can cleanse our hearts and minds as we respond to its commands.

Another way God's Word can help us is by answering the questions we all have, such as, "How can I be happy?" According to Psalm 119:14, you will find more enjoyment in God's Word than in all the riches of this world. Some people wonder how they can overcome depression. In Psalm 119:25 we read, "I am completely discouraged—I lie in the dust. Revive me by your Word" (TLB). Are you wondering about which way to go in life? We find our answer in Psalm 119:105: "Your word is a lamp to my feet and a light for my path."

The Benefits of Memorization

There are tremendous rewards available to the person who is willing to internalize God's Word. Storing God's Word in our mind aids in the process of seeking God, which is the central pursuit of the believer.[1] In Isaiah 55:1-6, the prophet asks, in essence, "Are you hungry or thirsty? Why do you work long hours and then spend your wages on things that do not satisfy you? Seek God while He may be found." Isaiah is pointing out that if a believer is not seeking God, he will be satisfied with nothing else and with nothing less. The place to seek God is in His Word, and the place where His Word is needed most is in your mind.

Stimulating your mind with the Scriptures will help keep you from wandering from God.[2] The psalmist knew his own tendency to stray, but he also was convinced that God's Word would bring him back. Written on the

front page of a famous preacher's Bible was this statement: "This Book will keep you from sin or sin will keep
you from this Book."

Let's try to recognize the opposition's strategy. In
Plan #1, Satan wants you to stay away from Scripture.
As we saw in 2 Corinthians 10:3-5, he desires to build
strongholds in your mind to keep out the knowledge of
God. If, however, you do read God's Word, then Plan #2
takes over—Satan tries to get you to forget what you
have read. The best defense against this tactic is to not
only read, but also *memorize* God's Word and let it take
root in your heart. When you do, you cause Satan to lose
his grip on you and your thinking.

How do you saturate yourself with God's Word? Let's
look at Psalm 119:11, a phrase at a time, for the answer:

> I have hidden your word [as we saw in the last
> chapter, only God's Word will do] in my heart.

We have a choice. We can either choose to *remember*
God's Word, or forget it. No one can remember it for us.
You can listen to the preaching of God's Word all your
life but unless you activate your will to remember (memorize), it will not have the effect God desires in your life.
Many Scripture passages warn us about the dangers of
forgetting. Psalm 106 describes how again and again
God's people forgot Him and all of His many kindnesses.[3]
God blessed Israel, "but they soon forgot what he had
done and did not wait for his counsel."[4] God told Moses
that the tendency would be to forget His commands and
decrees, challenging both Moses and the people to
remember in order to receive the promised blessings.[5]
As James 1:24 tells us, it is possible to look into God's
Word and then go away forgetting what we have read.
So the clear challenge is for us to remember the Word.

When the psalmist said, "I have hidden your word in my heart," literally, he was talking about storing up the Word. To hide God's Word in your heart is to carefully preserve it as you would a valuable treasure. Treat it as your prize possession by putting it right in the center of your thinking. Then when you need it, it will be there. Remember, your "heart" is the very center of who you are. You must hide His Word in the center of your being, where you reason, think, and determine to act.

The psalmist then shares the incredible benefit of memorizing God's Word, telling God he does this so that "*I might not sin against you.*" When God's Word takes up residence in your mind, it becomes a vital part of you. If you hide His Word in your heart, you will have a resource against sin (as we will see in a later chapter). But, if you don't hide God's Word in your heart, you will be prone to deception and sin. The Word dwelling in your mind and heart puts up a hedge against sinful thoughts and actions.

When you store Scripture in your mind, you will be able to retrieve it when you need it. Let's say, for instance, you are traveling on the highway and an inconsiderate driver crosses directly in front of you. Your foot slams on the brake and that hot cup of coffee splashes on the floor. In this age of "road rage," the temptation "to do likewise" immediately jumps into your mind. At that moment, what will you draw upon to counteract your impulse? It won't do any good to look at the billboards around you. Nor will it help to reach into the glove compartment. The only items there are gas receipts and maps. And you won't be able to open your Bible for help or you may very well end up off the road sightseeing in a farmer's field. The solution is to have God's Word already planted *in your heart.* At the moment you are cut off by another driver, if you have memorized

Ephesians 4:26, God will remind you, "In your anger do not sin."

Let's say you are at the doctor's office and you are overcome with fear concerning the prognosis of your illness. To your left lies *Time* magazine; on your right is the *Ladies Home Journal*. These are fine magazines, but they will not meet your need for comfort at that moment. God's Word will! The Holy Spirit can remind you of the promise in 2 Timothy 1:7, which says, "God did not give us a spirit of timidity, but a spirit of power, of love and of self-discipline."

Before we can apply God's Word to our life situations, we need to have it stored in our memories, ready to be brought back to our conscious mind when needed. Remember, Jesus said, "The Counselor, the Holy Spirit, whom the Father will send in my name, will teach you all things and will remind you of everything I have said to you" (John 14:26). The Spirit will remind us of what we have memorized just when we need it.

There are Christians who have survived extremely difficult circumstances and affirmed that it was the memorization of God's Word that pulled them through. I remember hearing a number of prisoners of war speak of how God's Word literally kept them from insanity while trapped in filthy, dark, cold cells. These prisoners were not allowed to possess a Bible, so all they had for their encouragement were the verses they had previously memorized.

Do you have large quantities of God's Word stored in your heart for the times when the written Word is unavailable? Right now is the time for you to be filling your mind with the only infallible source of information, the Bible. This was Paul's challenge when he said, "Let the word of Christ richly dwell *within you*" (Colossians 3:16 NASB).

Today, many different versions of the Bible are available to us. You'll want to choose the version that best suits your purpose in memorizing. Be careful to choose one that you can understand, and then begin memorizing Bible passages that are relevant to your life circumstances.

Ways to Remember God's Truth

There are several ways we can memorize information. The most commonly used method is *rote* memorization. This simply means you repeat the verse over and over again until you can finally recall it "automatically." As youngsters, this was the way we learned our multiplication tables.

With rote memorization it is important that you review regularly and recite the verses out loud. Carry cards on which you've written the Scriptures and look at them often. You may want to set the alarm on your watch to go off every hour so you can review your current memory verse at that time. The main drawback of using this method is that sometimes the thoughts behind the words being memorized are not always connected to the way in which we live. Consequently, much that is learned by rote can be quickly forgotten unless there is regular review and application.

Another way of memorizing verses is through *association*. This seems to have many advantages. One teacher, Jerry Lucas, has written a book entitled *Ready—Set—Remember.* Through different types of association techniques he suggests, we can remember full chapters and entire books. Most of us would admit that we don't have a "photographic memory," if there indeed is such a thing. But we do have minds that are capable of retaining mental pictures. Lucas said,

> I have never met a person with a photographic memory. Though many people have tried to credit me with that ability, it isn't true. If I had a photographic memory, I would be able to scan a page or several pages of printed material and make a mental photograph of the material. Later I would be able to recreate those printed pages in my mind and "read" the information as if the pages were before me. I can't do that, nor have I ever met anyone who could.
>
> I do have what I call a photographic mind. By that I mean that I can form mental images of persons or objects. But so can you! Every human being has that capacity.[6]

When we feel we just don't have what it takes to memorize Scripture, we need to remember Lucas' helpful illustration:

> It's as though there is a camera in your mind connected to a giant computer. Every time you think of an object, the computer causes the camera to duplicate and project it on a mental screen. It works automatically. It is a gift that God has given us all.[7]

We seem to best remember by association. When we are given instructions to a certain address and the instructions are just a list of street names and numbers, we aren't very likely to remember them. However, if someone tells us, "Turn left at the red barn, then right at the water tower. Then look for the blue house with orange trim," we will probably be able to reach our destination with little difficulty. That's because now we have visual images imprinted on our minds. Associating an object or visual image with a piece of information is a helpful way to make that information memorable.

One very helpful method of memorization is using music as a vehicle for words. Scripture songs, for instance, can be easily remembered because the words are linked with a memorable melody. There are already many Scripture songs available, but if you have some musical ability, you could compose your own tunes to accompany the Bible verses you wish to remember. And don't worry about whether you can sing; the music is a medium for memory, not a performance to be critiqued.

Sometimes an acrostic can be helpful. When I was taking piano lessons as a child, my teacher said I could remember the lines of the treble clef by reciting "Every Good Boy Does Fine." This little mnemonic device has helped me to remember that information to this day. In some Bible passages, the acrostic will be your best memory technique. For example, lists such as the one about the fruit of the Spirit can often be difficult to remember. However, if you just take the first letter of each of the fruit, you may be able to remember more easily. "The fruit of the Spirit is love, joy, peace, patience, kindness, goodness, faithfulness, gentleness and self-control" (Galatians 5:22-23). These letters form the acrostic LJPPKGFGS. You might form a silly word from this, such as Lejopipkegfigs, which hopefully would serve as a memory device to help you recite the fruit of the Spirit.

You may also find it helpful to write out the verse or passage you are memorizing. Somehow, when the words transfer from the Bible page through your pencil to the paper, they make a vivid impression on your thinking that is more apt to remain.

Maximizing Your Memorization

You should memorize when your mind is at its best. For some people, morning works better. For others, the evening hours are more suitable. I believe that is why God told Moses to talk about His words "when you lie down and when you get up."[8] Certainly God wanted people to talk about His Word so they would remember it. The moments before going to sleep or just after rising are a good time for us to focus on truth that will leave its imprint on our minds.

Don't try to memorize Scripture when you are physically drained. You'll find that more difficult, which could lead to real discouragement. Carry a card or small New Testament with you so you can glance at the verse or verses that you want to review. Whether you're in the doctor's office or waiting in line at the store or gas station, make use of the precious minutes that otherwise would be lost. Redeem the time and buy up opportunities for memorizing God's Word.[9] You will be amazed at how much time is actually available to be used in this profitable manner.

You may also find it very helpful to become accountable to someone. You could ask a friend to join you in memorizing God's Word and be willing to regularly ask one another to quote what you have memorized. Be careful, however, that you don't turn this activity into a competition. Let it simply be a time of encouraging one another in God's Word. Don't compete, just encourage. It is not how much Scripture you are memorizing, but rather that you are "hiding God's word in your heart" that counts. One verse a month is better than none at all.

I myself developed the habit of memorizing God's Word in an unexpected way. Immediately after I graduated from high school, I enlisted in the Army. Not many months later, I was transferred to Germany. The adjustment was very difficult for me. I experienced a combination of problems, including loneliness and temptation that seemed overpowering. Not knowing exactly how to respond, and at that time not yet acquainted with any Christians, I wrote my father in the States for counsel. With his answer, he sent among other things, the Navigators' *Topical Memory System.* I began to memorize God's Word as never before. I am convinced today that time of my life was a real turning point for me in my Christian experience. As I diligently endeavored to memorize the Word, God met my needs in wonderful ways. He brought within me a change of mind that benefited me greatly.

Taking the Step

Renewing the mind, then, is more than just gleaning information from God's Word. It's when we take that information and memorize it that Scripture is able to have a very real impact on our life. When we cultivate a regular habit of memorizing the Word, then we will have a wealth of truths and promises to draw upon for our moment-by-moment needs throughout the day.

God has given each of us the capability to memorize His Word. However, we must *choose* to hide it in our hearts. Will you commit yourself to taking this important step toward changing your mind and transforming your life? Why not choose a verse that has special meaning in your life right now and begin to memorize it? If you memorize just two verses per week, a year from now you could have more than 100 verses for whatever circumstances you might face—verses that can mean the difference between victory and defeat.

Would you like to unleash the power of God's Word in your life? All it takes to begin now is one verse.

Prayer

Father, help me to make time to memorize Your Word. I'm willing, Lord, by the power of Your Spirit, to start today. Thank You for the exciting potential I have in learning and obeying Your Word. In Christ's name, amen.

Success Unlimited

Meditation

Deanne sat uncomfortably in what was normally a comfy easy chair. Her mind raced from thought to thought and then back again in a seemingly endless circle. She mindlessly tapped her pencil on the pad of paper before her, on which she had written and crossed out many columns of numbers.

At first when their bills started piling up, they weren't concerned. But then a major blow came when Jim lost his job. It seemed so unfair after all the years of faithful service he had given to the company. Even though Jim was now drawing unemployment, the income was not sufficient to make ends meet. On top of all the other concerns, the doctor had just confirmed that their son, Shawn, would need surgery. It couldn't be postponed without danger to Shawn, but now there was no insurance and the medical costs would be astronomical.

Deanne looked again at the numbers, adding the savings to the checking account and subtracting the monthly bills. Yet again it did not work. Her mind retraced all the options as she felt herself breaking into tears.

The scenario I've just recounted is all too common in our pressured age. Medical problems, a lost job, and diminishing finances are the ingredients for stressful, worry-filled hours for many people. What's unfortunate, however, is that this troubled woman was using one of her God-given abilities to produce a worry-filled mind. She was *meditating* or dwelling on thoughts of worry. We may say she was actually expressing anxiety, but her thought process all started with meditation. The *content* of the meditation is what turned it into worry. We all have the ability to meditate either for good or for bad, which can affect the way we handle our circumstances.

Most believers, if asked to define meditation, would probably speak of Eastern gurus sitting cross-legged and glassy-eyed in silence. This is, in a sense, a true representation of something that purports to be meditation taught by Hindu mystics claiming to be nonreligious. Or, some may think of transcendental meditation (TM), which was once very popular and is frequently a part of relaxation techniques and exercise programs. Unfortunately, many who profess to be Christians have little understanding of true meditation and even less appreciation for its benefits.

What Is Biblical Meditation?

It might help us to recognize what meditation is not. Eastern meditation requires an emptying of the mind. The meditator uses a mantra—a mystical word or chant that is repeated over and over until all other thoughts are removed from the mind—to aid in his pursuit of revelations or insights, usually from an undefined source.

The caution expressed by Jesus in the following parable might be considered here:

> When an evil spirit comes out of a man, it goes through arid places seeking rest and does not find it. Then it says, "I will return to the house I left." When it arrives, it finds the house unoccupied, swept clean and put in order. Then it goes and takes with it seven other spirits more wicked than itself, and they go in and live there. And the final condition of that man is worse than the first. That is how it will be with this wicked generation (Matthew 12:43-45).

Clearing the mind of all rational thought is a most dangerous concept. Something must fill the space. The New Age technique of emptying the mind claims to produce some sort of pure awareness and a oneness with the absolute. These promises, however, are at best deceptive and at worst extremely dangerous. The meditator, rather than finding the God of the universe, discovers instead the gods of the demonic underworld.

In contrast to TM and other forms of non-Christian meditation, which persuade people to empty the mind and seek oneness with a "transcendent other," true biblical meditation fills the mind with truth. The purpose of this filling of the mind with God's thoughts is to leave no room for ideas that come from worldly sources.

Some believers express concern that people might use meditation as an escape from the pain and pressure of their busy lives. But the intent of meditation isn't to help a person escape from the distress of a divorce or the shock of a life-threatening illness and enter into a fantasy world. Rather, true meditation helps a person to apply biblical truth to difficult or stressful circumstances. Escape is not the goal, but rather, the ability to cope.

Some of the words that are descriptive of Christian meditation include *muse*, *reflect*, and even *ruminate*. Just as a cow first swallows what it eats and later regurgitates that food to give it another chew, so the Christian in his times of reflection swallows God's Word into his memory and then brings it back into his conscious mind again and again. Each new "chewing" yields even more of the nutrients that sustain spiritual life.

Meditation then, is simply the process of working biblical truth over and over in the mind so we can gain deeper insight into its meaning and make sure to apply it to our daily lives. J.I. Packer once said this about meditation:

> Meditation is the activity of calling to mind, and thinking over and dwelling on, and applying to oneself, the various things that one knows about the works and ways and purposes and promises of God.[1]

An interesting contrast surfaces when we consider the word *muse:*

> "Muse" was the name given to an ancient Greek god who spent much time in solitude and thinking.

> The statue of "The Thinker" is the artistic concept of deep concentration and absorption. Add an "a" to the beginning of "muse" and you have: "Amuse"—sports, games, television and a score of other tools used by the enemy to keep God's men from concentrating on man's God. [2]

Think for a moment about that statement: When we muse, we expend considerable mental energy. Our body may be at rest, but our mind is active and focused.

But when we are involved in amusements, often the opposite is true. We can vegetate before the television for hours without doing much thinking. When our amusement is done, we usually go away with little or nothing of lasting value. True meditation, by contrast, has far-reaching effects on us mentally, physically, emotionally, and spiritually.

Then there's the problem of musing upon the wrong information. Think back for a moment to Deanne, who was overwhelmed about her and Jim's financial situation. When Deanne was absorbed with worry, she was meditating—she was musing over her problems. Whatever it is that preoccupies our thoughts is the focus of our meditation. Our problem, then, is not understanding what meditation is; the real challenge is for us to meditate upon the right things.

Why Should We Meditate?

At a very critical moment in Israel's history, God spoke these words to Joshua:

> Do not let this Book of the Law depart from your mouth; meditate on it day and night, so that you may be careful to do everything written in it. Then you will be prosperous and successful (Joshua 1:8).

The emphasis here is that meditation is a discipline of the mind which bridges the gap between knowledge and action. Why are so many Christians knowledgeable and yet not experiencing God's truth? Because the truth has not taken root in their hearts through meditation. God desires for us to meditate on His Word "day and night, so that you may be careful to *do* everything written in it" (emphasis added).

A number of God's promises of blessing are directly linked to meditation. In Joshua 1:8, God says the result of meditating is both prosperity and success. Isn't that what each of us is looking for? The psalmist speaks of the same truth when he says that as a result of meditation, a person will prosper in "whatever he does" (Psalm 1:3).

What is prosperity? Is it wealth and fame? Not according to the Scripture. Many with wealth and fame have discovered with Solomon that even when "I became greater by far than anyone in Jerusalem before me . . . [and] when I surveyed all that my hands had done and what I had toiled to achieve, everything was meaningless, a chasing after the wind; nothing was gained under the sun."[3] True prosperity, declared the apostle Paul, is "godliness with contentment," which is "great gain."[4] And he explained the source of this contentment when he challenged Timothy to take pains to be absorbed in (meditate upon) the things of God.[5]

Many of us can easily be blinded by our own expectations and past experiences. We can be like the little girl who, upon traveling for the first time out of Brooklyn, viewed the cliffs and peaks of the Adirondack Mountains and exclaimed, "Mommy, look at the apartment house!" She assumed that everything that towered above her was an apartment building. Similarly, we tend to see prosperity as we have always been taught to see it through secular glasses. But it's vital for us to recognize that true prosperity goes far beyond the material and is available to us through biblical meditation.

According to Psalm 1, when we "walk in the counsel of the wicked or stand in the way of sinners or sit in the seat of mockers," the result will be a life of emptiness and insignificance. The input we receive from the world will leave us "like chaff that the wind blows away." On the other hand, when we meditate on God's Word, that meditation will lead us to godly actions, prosperity, and success as well as to true spiritual understanding. Meditation is an integral part of Christian growth and blessing.

Who Should Meditate?

Is meditation only for a few select "supersaints" or contemplative people? Not according to God's Word. The Lord calls for all of His people to meditate upon the law,[6] and He made His blessing dependent upon that. Every believer in Jesus Christ is indwelt by the Holy Spirit and has the Scriptures at his disposal. This combination makes *everything* necessary for life and godliness available to us.[7] Meditation is the method God has given us to draw upon the powerful resources of the Word and the Spirit, which give us wisdom and direction for life. No Christian can ignore meditation and expect to experience substantial growth and maturity!

When Should We Meditate?

Both Joshua and the psalmist emphasize that we are to meditate continuously. Joshua 1:8 exhorts us to "meditate on [God's Word] *day* and *night,"* and Psalm 1:2 repeats that truth.

This was undoubtedly a pattern of life for the biblical writers. Meditation, for them, was as natural as breathing. David F. Wells made this observation about the prophets of the Old Testament:

> The Spirit who made the prophets eloquent first of all made them thoughtful. In the later prophets especially, the Spirit first led them to ponder deeply the ways of God and the shortcomings of men. Then, when this reflective process came to maturity, they were ready to speak.[8]

As you look at your own life, do you recognize this kind of consistency in reflecting upon God's Word? Or do you fit into this description given by Malcolm Smith, who challenges our disorganized minds and harried lifestyles when he says:

> We are born into a rat race and inward silence appears as a mirage on the horizon of our minds. A bedlam of voices scream from within us, seeking to direct our actions. I took my puppy for a walk. He chased butterflies refusing to heed my call to heel, growled at rabbits that had outrun him into their warrens, and barked at any passing strangers. He lagged behind, investigating every scent on the breeze. I recognized my mind in the romping puppy. My thoughts will chase after every passing idea, bark angrily at all who outwit its wisdom or who seem to be trespassing on its rights and pursue every beckoning lust. Silence and stillness are the last arts my mind knows anything about.[9]

If we could count and record the thousands of thoughts and ideas that romp through our cluttered minds, how many of them could be classified as biblical meditation? Again, to quote Smith, "Meditation is waiting before the Word of God until it is heard with the ears within, and to go on to practice it until the whole lifestyle radiates God's thoughts."[10]

God's desire is that we wait before Him day and night in quiet reflection. We may turn our thoughts to Him and His Word at 2:00 A.M. when we are momentarily awakened from our sleep. We may reflect upon His precepts while commuting to work on the bus or standing in the grocery line. There will be those times when we specifically discipline our bodies and minds for meditation in a quiet place, but we must also snatch those brief moments of meditation from the center of our busiest hours. We must somehow break away from the rush and press long enough to establish a pattern of meditation that will include both the unhurried hours on the "mountain"[11] and the disciplined moments of reflection in the busy noise of the city.

What Should I Meditate Upon?

The Scriptures speak clearly about the content of our meditation. Simple alliteration might help us to remember the elements that ought to be present in our meditation: We are told to meditate upon God's *Works*, His *Ways,* and His *Word*.

The believer can reflect on the works of God by simply looking around him. In Psalm 8:3-4, we read:

> When I consider your heavens, the work of your fingers, the moon and the stars, which you have set in place, what is man that you are mindful of him, the son of man that you care for him?

Elsewhere, the psalmist declared, "I will meditate on all Thy work, and muse on Thy deeds,"[12] "They will speak of the glorious splendor of your majesty, and I will meditate on your wonderful works."[13] The beauties of God's creation present an undeniable witness to the character of the creator God.[14] A person can meditate upon the design of a snowflake, the color of a flower, or the amazing structure of the human body and recognize the orderliness and intricacy of creation. An awesome and powerful, yet sensitive God, is revealed in His universe.

In contrast to the meditative believer, the ungodly man refuses to recognize God in His works and foolishly worships the creation rather than the Creator.[15]

The ways of God are also food for meditation. We read in Psalm 119:15, "I meditate on your precepts and consider your ways." When we discover in Scripture how God has worked with others who have gone before us, we are able to understand how an unchanging God will deal with us. We see His many attributes revealed— such as holiness, kindness, justice, mercy, and love— and the more we know Him, the better we are able to serve and obey Him. Peter tells us that everything we will ever need in this life will be found in a knowledge of God,[16] and as we meditate upon His ways, that knowledge increases.

The Word of God is the central source of "information" for meditation. Psalm 119 repeats again and again, "I will meditate on your statutes," "your precepts," "your works," "your promises," and all that God's Word reveals.[17] This should take place even in negative circumstances when others speak against us (verse 23) and when they lie about us (verse 78) as well as in pleasant times because we "love Thy law" (verse 97 NASB). The Word of God should be our delight[18] in every instance and our constant companion both night[19] and day.[20]

The prideful man, by contrast, meditates upon himself, and the pessimistic man upon his problems. The prosperous man, however, meditates upon the works, ways, and Word of a sovereign God. The New Testament is equally clear about the content of our meditation. This is affirmed in Philippians 4:8, where Paul describes the information of our meditation as things that are true, noble, right, pure, lovely, and admirable. He then challenges us to discover anything excellent and praiseworthy and make these things the food for our constant thought.

Where Do I Begin?

It is possible to recognize the potential of meditation and still not meditate. It is evident that God wants us to be reflective people, but often the desire for this sort of discipline is absent. David F. Wells comments insightfully:

> There seems to be a vicious circle involved in this. We do not reflect on God unless we desire to do so; we do not desire to do so unless we habitually reflect on Him. There is no easy way into this circle. The desire for God does not appear overnight like the desert bloom. It is, like all life, fragile in its infancy. Like a newborn child, it has to be carefully tended, nourished and trained. Reflection leads to desire and desire stimulates reflection. The utter seriousness of this quest, however, cannot be diluted.[21]

With these words in mind, we are back to the necessity of the step of obedience. We may not feel like meditating, but that feeling will never arise unless we choose to meditate. Simply put, we must begin by taking the first step, regardless of our feelings.

Step by Step

Let's review the first three steps in renewing the mind. If you have a problem area in your life, you first need the correct "information" from God's Word concerning your difficulty. You then need to "memorize" the information and use it as fuel for your "meditation." If, for example, you have a problem with worry, you might begin with Matthew 6:25-34. Each day you could carefully read and inductively study the passage. You could memorize one or more of the key verses in order to carry them along in your mind throughout the day. As suggested earlier, you could use an alarm on your watch or another form of reminder to cause you to consciously meditate upon the principles every few hours throughout the day. Every worrisome or unacceptable thought could be used as a reminder to *recognize*, *recapture*, *refuse,* and then *replace* your thought with God's information, which you would then meditate upon.

The more we consciously discipline ourselves to study, memorize, and meditate in this way, the more habitual it will become. Eventually, we will awaken even in the "night watches" with God's thoughts before us.

Putting Down Your Roots

A number of years ago, my wife and I were walking along the Oregon coast enjoying its beauty when we came upon a huge tree lying across the path. The tree must have been nearly 60 feet in length, but its root system was very shallow. The heavy winds off the ocean the night before had been too much for the feeble roots and the tree had toppled.

Many of us as Christians are much like that tree. We have been believers for a number of years, but our root system is so weak that adverse winds are continually blowing us over. Meditation is God's method of helping us to cultivate healthy roots which reach deep into the fertile soil of His truth.

The psalmist says this of the person who meditates on God's truth: "He is like a tree planted by streams of water, which yields its fruit in season and whose leaf does not wither. Whatever he does prospers."[22]

If your true desire is to be like that fruit-bearing tree, your next step is meditation.

Prayer

Father, thank You for the truth of Your Word and for the privilege of being able to take it with me wherever I go. In my hands and in my heart, help me, Lord, to meditate on it by the power of Your Spirit. In Jesus' name, amen.

Imagine That!

Imagination

One cold, crisp fall day in October, my father took me duck hunting for a weekend. We slept overnight in our station wagon and got up an hour before dawn to watch for ducks beside a small, secluded lake. Five hours later we hadn't seen a single duck, and I was restless! I asked my father if I could walk back along the logging road to see if I might scare up a partridge or two. He agreed, and after about a mile of walking, still in my heavy hip boots, I discovered another small road. Thinking it looked interesting, I decided to follow along its course only to discover that it gradually narrowed to a foot path. That path led me to a marshy area, heightening my hopes that at any moment I would surprise a partridge!

I lost all track of how far I had gone, and soon realized I'd also left solid ground. I was surrounded by water. Nearby, I discovered a leaf-covered ridge of land. Stopping to rest before heading back, I leaned against a small tree. In the breathtaking quietness of my surroundings,

I heard footsteps up on the ridge—crunch! . . . crunch! I listened, but all I could hear was the heavy pounding of my heart . . . crunch! . . . crunch! I knew it couldn't be a squirrel or a deer, for the rhythmic noise was made by something navigating on two feet—heavy feet at that! Straining to see through the trees, I took a breath ever so quietly. Then an idea hit me: If it was a man, he would answer me.

"Hello, there!" I shouted. But it was still silent, and the crunching sound continued.

"Who is it?" my feeble voice asked, barely audible this time. Still, no answer.

Though I could see nothing, my imagination began to run wild. Perhaps it was a hungry bear silently preparing to make me the main course for his noon meal! My pulse rate climbed so high that I was sure the approaching creature could hear my heart thumping! By now I was convinced it was a bear, and the old 12-gauge shotgun, hanging limp in my hand feeling like a small pea shooter, gave me no confidence in this terrifying situation.

One more crunch sent me gulping for a deep breath and off I ran, sloshing through the mud, water, and underbrush, adrenaline pumping through my veins like hot lava! What a sight I must have been, leaving a trail behind me looking as though a locomotive had steamed through! Never glancing back, I fixed my attention on one purpose: getting away from the reach of that treacherous bear! I don't believe I ever exerted more energy in my life. Today I still wonder if I didn't run the first four-minute mile in hip boots!

Now, you may be asking, "Did you ever see the bear?" No, at least not with my eyes. But my imagination had made him so real I hadn't needed any visual contact. That day, I recognized in my own experience a truth that has since become an important factor in my Christian life: Our God-given ability to imagine has just as powerful an influence on our actions as does the actual experience. In fact, there are some who say that the human nervous system cannot tell the difference between an actual experience and an experience we vividly imagine.

On that memorable day in the swamp, I had so clearly imagined the bear's existence that all my faculties were tuned to one goal: self-preservation. I never will know if that really was a bear; yet, I reacted exactly as if it had been.

Completing the Bridge

What does all this have to do with changing our minds and transforming our lives? It demonstrates an important principle: Your imagination, in conjunction with biblical meditation, *completes* the bridge between God's truth and godly actions. Before you do something, it helps you to have a clear picture in your mind of what successful completion would look like. Imagination precedes application.

Webster defines *imagination* as "the act or power of forming mental images of what is not present." It is the God-given ability to visualize something in the mind *as if it were so*. Whether or not your perception of a given situation is correct, you will respond according to what you imagine to be true.

Before we go any further, a warning is in order here. Today, New Age advocates, faith movement teachers, and psychologists have also discovered the importance of the imagination. In those circles, this is commonly called *guided imagery* or *visualization*. It may sound harmless, but because the human imagination is marred by sin (see Genesis 6:5), it's possible for imagination to be used wrongly with dangerous consequences. Many of the ideas and practices of these people have been far from the biblical teaching concerning the imagination. I will try in the coming pages to steer this discussion carefully through what could be treacherous waters. On the one hand, we must avoid the potentially destructive rocks of confusion, and on the other, we want to discover the biblically charted route that will help us reach our destination.

Far more complex than a computer, the mind is an amazing organ that retains what you put into it. If you program your "computer" with incorrect thoughts about life, it will faithfully replay those false images. Your imagination is actively involved in that programming. It is much more difficult to edit and delete information once it has already been entered into your thinking. Your response to life is directly linked to how you have programmed your mind.

The "Heart" of Things

The Bible often speaks of the imaginations, inclinations, or intentions of the heart. When Scripture speaks of the heart, it's frequently referring to the center of your thinking and acting. You imagine, reason, rationalize, and decide with your "heart." Just a reminder here: Don't confuse the biblical heart with the idea that our emotions originate there. Primarily thinking, not feeling, takes place in your "heart."[1]

Of course, the heart is capable of both negative and positive imagination. We read in Genesis 6:5 that in Noah's time, "the LORD saw that the wickedness of man was great on the earth, and that every intent of the thoughts of his heart was only evil continually" (NASB). At that point in history, people's imaginations were totally wicked!

> When the noun *yeser* is used in Genesis 6:5 of the imagination (NIV=inclination) of the thoughts of

the heart, it describes. . .the fashioning of an idea within one's mind. It is the image-making capacity of the inner man, imitative of the activity of God, for evil or for good.[2]

Ezekiel records one of the lowest moral points in Israel's history when he says that the elders were committing gross sin in the dark, "each at the shrine of his own idol."[3] Both in their imaginations and in their actions they were idol worshipers. The imaginations of our hearts can be rooms filled with idols, or they can be sanctuaries set apart for the worship of a holy God. Os Guinness warns us of the idol-making propensity of the imagination when he says:

Idols are nonexistent, mere fictions, false gods. But this knowledge by itself is not a safeguard against idolatry because it is not a stand-alone truth. It requires both an accompanying call to love and obedience, as well as the reminder that the imagination of our sinful hearts has such a reality-creating power that the nonexistent is invested with its own dynamic. Thus, regardless of what the mind "knows," the imagination of the heart can change the mind. It can turn lies into truth, fictions into reality, no-gods into gods, and the quite incredible into the utterly credible. This idol-making propensity of the imagination of our hearts is a continuing and deadly threat to faith. Having once turned from idols to the living God, our task of keeping on turning is never done.[4]

The psalmist writes of the wicked when he says, "Their eye bulges from fatness; the imaginations of their heart run riot."[5] Apart from God's power and control, the imagination can run wild. Jesus speaks of this when He teaches His disciples about lust:

> You have heard that it was said, "Do not commit
> adultery." But I tell you that anyone who looks at
> a woman lustfully has already committed adul-
> tery with her in his heart (Matthew 5:27-28).

It hardly seems fair to equate *imagined* adultery with
the real thing, but Jesus does not differentiate between
the two. Why? Because imagination *precedes* action.
What you think, you will eventually act out. Jesus also
said that whatever is in our hearts is an indicator of our
true condition, or who we really are: "The good man
brings good things out of the good stored up in his
heart, and the evil man brings evil things out of the evil
stored up in his heart. For out of the overflow of his
heart his mouth speaks" (Luke 6:45). What you imagine
is not really as secret as you might believe, for your
secret thoughts will eventually reveal themselves in
your public personality and performance.

The writer of Proverbs tells of a man who finds his
security in what he imagines: "The wealth of the rich is
their fortified city; they imagine it an unscalable wall"
(Proverbs 18:11). We know that to base our future on
wealth rather than on God is foolish. However, in this
man's imagination, his riches are like a high wall which
he thinks will protect him from any calamity.

Daydreams?

Let's clarify one possible misunderstanding. When I
speak of the wise use of the imagination, I am not referring to either daydreaming or fantasy. Both of these are
improper uses of a God-given ability. Daydreaming is an
escape from reality that seldom has any beneficial
results. Fantasy is an illusion of a reality rather than a
mental image of what is or can be. Fantasy will have us
walking on the moon, while proper use of the imagination will help us to walk carefully so as to make the most

of our time.[6] As Malcolm Smith stated, our imagination can be used or abused:

> Each of us has a movie theater within the mind where we play out our meditation dramas: the theater of the imagination. It is here that we re-enact the hurts inflicted on us, the wrong done to us whether real or imagined. We play the words, the incidents, the looks people give us, over and over again until we are wallowing in the dismal swamp of bitterness and hate; all our thoughts caught in its foul slime and odor.
>
> In that same theater we play out our lusts, our plans of impurity and greed. Every impure act, every lie told is first rehearsed on that stage. It is here, as we cast our characters, that we choose who we shall be in our tomorrow.
>
> All our worries and fears begin as we write the script of the days to come. We play the tragic hero caught in the hopeless set of circumstances we create.[7]

The abuse of the imagination results in negative and destructive behavior, while the wise use of the imagination will bring positive benefits. However, understanding and properly using the imagination is not simply a technique of "positive thinking." Rather, it is a part of God's design which makes it possible for us to anticipate what could be. It was said of Stephen Charnock, the writer of the great Christian classic *The Existence and Attributes of God,* that:

> His fine and teeming imagination, ever under the strict control of reason and virtue, was uniformly turned to the most important purposes. This department of mental phenomena, from the abuses to which it is liable, is apt to be undervalued; yet, were this the proper place, it would

not be difficult to show that imagination is one of
the noblest faculties with which man has been
endowed—a faculty, indeed, the sound and
proper use of which is not only necessary to the
existence of sympathy and other social affec-
tions, but also intimately connected with those
higher exercises of soul, by which men are
enabled to realize the things that are not seen
and eternal. Charnock's imagination was under
the most cautious and skillful management—the
handmaid, not the mistress of his reason.[8]

In his lexicon, J. H. Thayer explains a word that will
help our understanding here. In 2 Corinthians 4:18, two
types of vision are mentioned: We as believers can see
what is seen, and we can see what is not seen. That is,
we can see with the eyes and see with the imagination:

Our light and momentary troubles are achieving
for us an eternal glory that far outweighs them
all. So we fix our eyes not on what is seen, but on
what is unseen. For what is seen is temporary, but
what is unseen is eternal (2 Corinthians 4:17-18).

Four times, a more common Greek word is used in
reference to what is seen or unseen. However, there also
appears a less-common Greek word that is translated
"fix our eyes." Thayer says we can read that word to
mean "fixing one's *mind's* eye upon" something.[9] We as
believers cannot only see the temporal things that are
visible to the human eye, but we can also see the eternal
things that are visible to an imagination that has been
nourished by God's Word.

To ignore your imagination, then, in the pursuit of a
renewed mind would be foolish. Rather, I would challenge you to exercise it for your own benefit and
blessing. Ron Allen says:

The same word that describes the ability of the human mind to pervert, distort and ruin a sense of reality is also used in the Bible to describe deep devotion and piety to God. Isaiah does this in a text beloved by many people: "You will keep in perfect peace him whose mind is steadfast, because he trusts in you" (Isaiah 26:3). Here the word translated "mind" is *yeser* (imagination), the same term we found in Genesis 6:5 used for evil imagination. But in this case, Isaiah says that the imagination of the righteous is "steadfast." This adjective places some form of restraint upon the imagination, a restraint only upon evil impulse. That is, we may say that this verse describes *imagination that is under discipline*. This kind of imagination is born of confident faith in Yahweh and results in sublime peace— the peace that comes only from God.[10]

Imagination in Action

When you look back at your life, you are "reviewing" your past actions. When you use your imagination properly, you are "previewing" your future actions. This previewing can be a means of preparing your thinking for success in your spiritual growth.

Training your mind to think a new way is not an instantaneous occurrence. It takes exercise and practice. Paul told Timothy not to waste his time with worldly things but to "discipline [exercise or train] yourself for the purpose of godliness" (1 Timothy 4:7 NASB). The writer to the Hebrews describes mature believers as those "who because of practice have their senses trained to discern good and evil" (Hebrews 5:14 NASB). The word "trained" here is the same as the one in 1 Timothy 4:7, but the "practice" spoken of is defined as "a habit of body or mind, a power acquired by custom, practice and use."[11]

Developing godly habits by the proper use of your imagination takes time and exercise. It is common knowledge that it usually requires a minimum of about 21 days to effect any perceptible change in a mental image. When an arm or leg is amputated, the "phantom limb" persists for about 21 days. People must live in a new house for about three weeks before it begins to "seem like home." These and many other commonly observed phenomena tend to show that it requires a period of time for an old mental image to dissolve and a new one to jell.

For example, if I now brush my teeth with my right hand and wish to change and use my left hand, I must make a conscious effort to remember to pick up my toothbrush with my left hand every time. If I continue to do that, within about three weeks I will begin to automatically pick up the brush with my left hand rather than my right. If I persist in doing this for another three weeks, I will have formed a new habit that replaces the old.

Have you ever resolved to spend more time with God, wanting to have a more meaningful prayer life and more in-depth time in His Word? Perhaps you've had times when you tried to get up a half-hour earlier than usual to do so. But after a few days of success, you may have found yourself lapsing back into your old habits, and filled with feelings of guilt because you didn't do better. Don't let that discourage you. The important principle is this: You must endeavor to persist for at least three weeks before you will find your new habit falling naturally into place.

In the same way, we must reprogram our imaginations according to God's Word if we are to be "conformed to the image" of Christ.[12] Over the years, we have been programmed by numerous sources of influence and may have picked up opinions, thoughts, or ideas that don't agree with the Scriptures. In order to change our thinking, we first need the correct *information*. Secondly, we must feed that information into our mind through *memorization*. We then need, from time to time, to pull those memorized truths out into our conscious mind to reflect on them in *meditation*. Then we can act out these godly principles on the screen of our *imagination* and see ourselves obeying God's truth. These mental images of obedience turn programmed truth into processed truth. Imagination directs God's principles into living, breathing actions.

Picturing Your Future

Let's use our imaginations right now by taking a passage of God's Word and applying it. Philippians 4:6 reads, "Be anxious for nothing, but in everything by prayer and supplication with thanksgiving let your requests be made known to God" (NASB). Remember, as we learned earlier, we act and feel according to how we perceive things to be. If I believe my circumstances are beyond God's control, I will live as if they are and I'll worry. But if I believe that God will take care of me in the midst of my circumstances and picture myself obeying Him, I will not be anxious. If I see myself as a man of prayer who lets all his requests be made known to a God who promises peace, I will experience His peace. If I will persistently turn to God in prayer each time my worries arise, He will respond to my obedience by guarding my heart and mind from worry.

You may say, "I've tried that, but it didn't work!" Did you persist for at least three weeks in praying to God each time you recognized a worrisome thought? If not, you haven't given your God-designed imagination the opportunity to reprogram your worry-filled mind.

When you imagine yourself obeying God's Word, you are not relying on the "power of positive thinking," but on the power of biblical thinking. Those who promote the idea of positive thinking tend to emphasize the use of the mind to *escape* reality and often become very self-focused in the pursuit of personal and material success. For the believer, the use of the mind and imagination is to be Christ-centered, biblically based, and focused on applying God's principles for living successfully in the real world. It is not a matter of psyching yourself up, using guided imagery or visualizations; but rather, you are simply picturing and then acting out the truth in obedience.

But Will It Work?

A research quarterly reported an experiment in which people were asked to throw a basketball through a hoop while standing at the free-throw line on a basketball court. Three groups of students were asked to take part. One group practiced throwing the ball every day for 20 days and were scored on the first and last days of the experiment. A second group was scored on the first and last days and engaged in no sort of practice in between. A third group was scored on the first day, then spent 20 minutes a day imagining that they were throwing the ball at the hoop. When they missed, they would imagine that they corrected their aim accordingly.

The first group, which actually practiced 20 minutes every day, improved in scoring 24 percent. The second group, which had no sort of practice, showed no improvement. The third group, which practiced in their imagination, improved in scoring 23 percent! Imagination accomplished substantially as much as actual practice!

If you will begin to use your imagination as a Spirit-directed tool for Christian growth, you will experience similar results. Old habits will be replaced and new ones formed. Areas of failure will be transformed into victories. Best of all, your mind will be renewed with exciting results!

Prayer

Dear Lord, I want to thank You for the wonderful way in which You designed my mind. I recognize that I have often used my imagination for evil, and I confess that as sin. By Your power, I now desire to use my imagination as a tool for spiritual growth. Help me to persist in developing my imagination in biblical ways. In Jesus' name, amen.

Buried Treasure

Application

Imagine that a trustworthy friend of yours came to you with news about a discovery he made. Recently, he purchased a cabin in the foothills of the Sierra Nevada Mountains in California. While cleaning one of the rooms, he found a small box in the corner. Curious to know what was in it, he gingerly opened the dust-covered container. To his surprise, he found a weathered map. Carefully he unfolded it, examined it, and found that it gave directions to buried treasure on a nearby mountain. Knowing you to be an adventurous soul, he decided to ask you if you would be interested in going with him to hunt for the treasure.

A few days after accepting this invitation, you and your friend head up into the mountains. After several hours of difficult climbing, you struggle to get over the last rocky path and arrive at the peak to find the hiding place well marked. Tingling with excitement, both of you dig swiftly, using a pick and shovel. Sure enough, you find an old chest in the ground. Holding your breath in anticipation, you break the rusty lock, open the lid, and see millions of dollars in gold coins! Then, after the excitement of the discovery wears off, the two of you decide to bury the treasure back in the ground and return home with no intention of digging it up again.

If that had really happened, would you have reburied the treasure?

Imagine yourself in another scenario. Several months ago the weather was so beautiful that you determined to work out in the yard to achieve the impossible all in one afternoon. Because of your zealous attitude, you overworked yourself and later that evening, you begin to feel a strange numbness creeping up your legs. Dismissing it as the result of overactivity, you swallowed two aspirin, took a hot shower, and climbed into bed. By morning, however, the numbness had not disappeared; rather, it had spread to your arms and was now accompanied with pain. After several days of this, you decided to notify your family doctor. He, too, attributed your condition to your activity in the garden. Still, the pain and numbness persisted. But you persevered until one day, one of your limbs suddenly became limp. Wasting no time, you called an extremely qualified diagnostician and set up an appointment. After a great deal of careful testing, he informed you that you had acquired a rare disease with only one known cure. To your delight and relief, a miracle drug specifically designed to cure this disease had been discovered only a few months earlier. The doctor wrote out the prescription, gave you explicit instructions for its usage, and sent you on your way. After you picked up the medication from the pharmacist, you went home, walked into the bathroom, and placed the medicine in the cabinet above the sink—with no plans to ever take it.

If you really had become afflicted with a life-threatening disease, would you have ignored the one medication that could cure it?

Consider one more situation. You are a believer in Christ and have a sincere desire to know what God wants for your life. To aid you in your pursuit, God has revealed a way to discover His perfect will. He has given you a spiritual road map with each turn carefully marked. After looking at the map for a few minutes, you put it away in a drawer, never to look at it again.

Do you see a pattern developing in all those scenarios? It would be ludicrous to discover gold and then to rebury it, and absolutely foolish to possess a medication that could cure your terminal disease and refuse to take it. It would be no less absurd to have God's divine road map, the Bible, in your possession and yet ignore its application in your life.

Knowing and Doing

The apostle James said it so clearly: "Prove yourselves *doers* of the word, and not merely hearers who delude themselves" (James 1:22 NASB, emphasis added). It is wonderful for us to have God's *information* to give us guidance. It is even more beneficial if we *memorize* His information and *meditate* upon it day and night. The blessings multiply when we *imagine* ourselves living in obedience to the truth, thereby firmly fixing that truth in our minds. But the cycle is incomplete until we have *applied* the truth to our life. British theologian John Stott wrote, "Knowledge carries with it the solemn responsibility to act on the knowledge we have, to translate our knowledge into appropriate behavior."[1] He also said, "God never intends knowledge to be an end in itself but always to be a means to some other end."[2]

In Deuteronomy chapters 5–6, no less than 13 challenges are given to observe, keep, or walk in God's commandments. The overriding emphasis is upon the application of God's truth to life. For example, Moses said:

> Be careful to do what the LORD your God has commanded you; do not turn aside to the right or to the left. Walk in all the way that the LORD your God has commanded you, so that you may live and prosper and prolong your days in the land that you will possess (Deuteronomy 5:32-33).

Moses told the people that God commanded him to teach them the statutes so they might observe and obey them.[3] He promised a number of positive results when they applied God's truth to their lives. First, in Deuteronomy 6:1-2, he said this obedience will bring about a reverence for God, which in turn will result in a greater obedience and will prolong their lives. Some Christians appear to be waiting for a lightning bolt to strike them from heaven before they can be sure God has spoken. But Moses' teaching is very clear: We are called to obey what we already know from God's Word—then God will reveal more to our understanding. Why should God give us the second half of the map when we haven't followed the first part?

Another positive result of being doers and not hearers only is that our lives will serve as a witness to unbelievers. A life lived in obedience can become a platform from which to proclaim the truth of Jesus Christ. The world must first see the message of our lives before they will listen to the words from our lips.

The Happy Home

In Deuteronomy 6, Moses also spoke of applying God's truth in the home. Verse 7 says we are to teach God's words in our home and talk of them. The Lord's desire for a Christian home is that His Word pervade every aspect of family life. Application of the Word is to take place "when you sit at home and when you walk along the road" (Deuteronomy 6:7). It is not only to take place during a specified time for family devotions, but even in times of recreation, relaxation, or relating to one another. It is to be integrated with all your family activities even "when you lie down and when you get up" (verse 7). The last thought at night and the first in the morning should be centered on God's truth and its application.

This living application of God's truth is to reach out into the community as well. It is to affect the people of your neighborhood because each individual within the family has bound God's Word as a "symbol" on his hand and forehead (verse 8). In other words, the revelation of God's truth through each family member's life can serve as a powerful witness to others. The whole family can have a corporate witness to a watching world.

Some years ago when our family moved into a new neighborhood, word got around quickly that I was a pastor. We knew this meant we would have to progress very carefully in our relationships with the neighbors so that we wouldn't immediately turn anyone off. Our six year-old son, on the other hand, didn't feel the same hesitation. The neighbors next door were cordial, but we could sense they were a little afraid of us. Our son wasn't about to let that stop him. One day while the wife was working in her garden, our son walked over and struck up a conversation. She was still cautious toward me and my wife, but she immediately connected with our son. They became fast friends. Shortly afterwards, she introduced our son to her husband and they hit it off as well. Now that our son had opened the door, they warmed up to us and a friendship developed. Not many months later, my wife was able to share Christ with the wife and she received Jesus as her Savior. The husband was slower to respond, but eventually he trusted Christ as well.

The verses we just looked at in Deuteronomy 6 came to my mind as I thought of that experience. Our son, in his childlike faith, was not hesitant to wear God's truth as a "symbol on his forehead." His friendly, childlike approach to our neighbors signaled for them that God's Word was also a part of our lives. Your application of God's principles in your family life will be like writing them "on the doorframes of your houses and on your gates" (Deuteronomy 6:9).

Follow-Through

For two years, I worked in the summer months as a greenskeeper on a golf course. I had the opportunity to watch countless people become frustrated as they flailed at a little white ball, which made me a confirmed non-golfer. On one particular ladies' day while I sat on my riding mower beside an apron, I observed two women playing: one a very tense novice, and the other a more experienced golfer. As the beginner prepared to tee off, her mentor said, "Now, don't forget to follow through so you won't put the ball in the woods again!" Needless to say, the novice did exactly that—her ball ended up right in the center of the woods. As I watched, I thought about what the other woman had said about following through. She had touched upon the greatest weakness of my Christian experience: I knew a good deal of God's truth, but I wasn't following through and applying it to my everyday experience.

"Follow through" is really what James meant when he challenged us to be "doers of the Word."[4] He illustrated his point by speaking of a man who looks in a mirror and sees himself as he really is. How do you look when you first get up in the morning? Is your hair in disarray, and are there circles under your eyes? Perhaps you feel as if the little blood vessels in your eyes look like a map of the canal system in Venice. Whatever the case, as you stand before the mirror, the truth is mercilessly unveiled before your eyes. Now, let's say you turn away and make no attempt to reconstruct yourself, singing, "Oh, what a handsome specimen am I!" on the way to the breakfast table. You'd be deceiving yourself, wouldn't you?

The Word of God is like that mirror. It tells us the stark truth about ourselves and pulls no punches. It also explains what to do about what we see. But, we begin to delude ourselves when we turn from the Word of God and refuse to act on what we have read. James recites the blessing of applying the truth when he says, "The man who looks intently into the perfect law that gives freedom, and continues to do this, not forgetting what he has heard, but doing it—he will be blessed in what he does" (James 1:25).

Foundation Stones

Jesus tells a very important story at the end of His powerful Sermon on the Mount.[5] After presenting a description of kingdom living, He applies His teaching. We know that the content of His sermon was very effective because Matthew tells us, "When Jesus had finished saying these things, the crowds were amazed at his teaching, because he taught as one who had authority, and not as their teachers of the law" (Matthew 7:28-29).

Jesus' application was a parable about two builders, one wise and one foolish. Let's read the parable in Matthew 7:24-27:

> Everyone who hears these words of mine and puts them into practice is like a wise man who built his house on the rock. The rain came down, the streams rose, and the winds blew and beat against that house; yet it did not fall, because it had its foundation on the rock. But everyone who hears these words of mine and does not put them into practice is like a foolish man who built his house on sand. The rain came down, the streams rose, and the winds blew and beat against that house, and it fell with a great crash.

The difference between the wise person and the foolish is that the wise person hears what Jesus has said and responds, while the foolish one hears but ignores His words.

The person whom Jesus declared to be wise was a sensible, practical individual. The other person was called foolish, and the word used in the original Greek text is similar to our English word *moron*—not a very complimentary description.

Both individuals built houses, and we can assume they appeared very similar. They evidently had good materials and used quality construction techniques. If an observer had given both houses a cursory look, it would have been difficult to tell them apart. The main difference was the two foundations. The wise builder constructed his house upon a solid rock, while the foolish man built his on the sand.

A number of years ago a church I pastored in Northern California was considering building a new auditorium. The site was in a very beautiful area called the Oakland Hills. Architects from Michigan were hired to design the building. The problem was that they did not understand the inherent instability of the hillside upon which the auditorium was to be built. When the plans were finished, everyone was impressed. However, when the plans were put out for bids from the local construction companies, the shock came. The estimated cost was more than double what we expected because the local builders knew the need for a much more extensive foundation. The building could not be built on unstable soil; it had to be connected to bedrock. Sadly, the beautiful plans were put in a closet, where they remain today because the architects, who were from outside California, hadn't known what kind of foundation would be necessary for the building.

In Christ's parable, the foolish man was like those architects. He didn't allow for a proper foundation; he built his house on shifting sands.

The foolish man's folly would never have played out if it had not been for the storm that soon came. It was the storm that revealed the inadequate foundation. What's more, the original Greek text tells us that the storms in the parable were not the same. The rains and wind that buffeted the house on the rock were much stronger than the storm that hit the house on the sand. The house on the rock faced gale-force winds and raging floods—yet it still stood. By contrast, the storm that battered the house on the sand was not as powerful, and Jesus said, "It fell with a great crash."

Many Christians build their lives in ways that appear to be beneficial and yet, when the storms come, their lives collapse in ruin. Why? Because of the foundation upon which they choose to build. A believer may appear to be very successful in all he does, but if he's not building on the right foundation, his success won't last.

Jesus clearly tells us which kind of foundation will be sufficient for the challenges of life. The wise man hears God's Word and puts it into practice, while the foolish man hears God's Word, but does not apply it to his life.

The question we should ask ourselves is this: Do I hear and obey God's truth, or do I hear and ignore it? That will tell you what kind of foundation you're building on. All of the steps that we have discussed for mind renewal will fall short of the goal unless this last step is followed.

Jesus' illustration is very pertinent to our discussion. Our lives will not be on a solid foundation just because we know God's Word. Those foundation stones are properly laid when we both *know* and *do* what God says. Simply said, our spiritual house will withstand the floods of circumstances when we are regularly applying God's precepts to our daily experience.

Application Applied

Application is a very practical thing, so let's apply what we are learning right now. Say, for example, you have a problem with the misuse of your tongue in the area of gossip or harsh criticism. The first step is to get God's *information* on this subject. You might look at Romans 1:29, where the gossiper is listed along with murderers and deceivers. That may seem strong; but, remember, the mirror only reflects the truth about us. Second Corinthians 12:20 lists some specific misuses of the tongue:

> I am afraid that when I come I may not find you as I want you to be, and you may not find me as you want me to be. I fear that there may be quar-

reling, jealousy, outbursts of anger, factions, slander, gossip, arrogance and disorder.

James 3:3-12 is very helpful, giving us some words about the power of the tongue:

> When we put bits into the mouths of horses to make them obey us, we can turn the whole animal. Or take ships as an example. Although they are so large and are driven by strong winds, they are steered by a very small rudder wherever the pilot wants to go. Likewise the tongue is a small part of the body, but it makes great boasts. Consider what a great forest is set on fire by a small spark. The tongue also is a fire, a world of evil among the parts of the body. It corrupts the whole person, sets the whole course of his life on fire, and is itself set on fire by hell. All kinds of animals, birds, reptiles and creatures of the sea are being tamed and have been tamed by man, but no man can tame the tongue. It is a restless evil, full of deadly poison. With the tongue we praise our Lord and Father, and with it we curse men, who have been made in God's likeness. Out of the same mouth come praise and cursing. My brothers, this should not be. Can both fresh water and salt water flow from the same spring? My brothers, can a fig tree bear olives, or a grapevine bear figs? Neither can a salt spring produce fresh water.

There is no doubt that an evil use of the tongue is sin; still, you need even more information than that. A key verse on the tongue, Ephesians 4:29, says, "Do not let any unwholesome talk come out of your mouths, but only what is helpful for building others up according to their needs, that it may benefit those who listen."

Your second step, *memorization*, involves taking verses like Ephesians 4:29 and Psalm 141:3 ("Set a guard over my mouth, O LORD; keep watch over the door of my lips") and begin to memorize them. Write out the verses on a card and carry them wherever you go. Follow some of the memory techniques mentioned in chapter six and hide these words of God in your heart.

The third step in the process is *meditation*. You can begin this step even while you are memorizing. In chapter three, we looked at four words that can help aid us in reprogramming our thinking: *recognize, recapture, refuse,* and *replace*. You'll find this pattern useful in your meditation. When a situation arises during your day and you are about to say something unkind or sinful, you can recognize and recapture the thought, refuse it, and call Ephesians 4:29 to memory and dwell upon it. When you meditate upon God's truth, it will become a part of you.

The fourth step is *imagination*. How would Christ Himself deal with this circumstance? Can you picture His response? Then imagine yourself responding to the difficult situations of your life just as He would, according to God's Word. For example, there may be a certain individual with whom you regularly gossip. You know it's wrong and so does your friend, but you have developed a habit that is now a part of your relationship. Spend time imagining yourself responding differently the next time you have an opportunity to gossip with this person. Picture yourself speaking wholesome truths and redirecting the conversation to words that are helpful for building others up. See yourself as a person who can move the conversation from gossip to grace for those who hear.

The final step in this process is *application*. This is the place where the blade meets the ice. Let's say that tomorrow morning you will see your friend and have an opportunity to build him up or break him down. The choice is yours. You could take up where you left off and allow your tongue to be a razor used to dissect others, or you could redirect the conversation in obedience to God's principle and give a word that benefits those who listen.

Let's assume the conversation drifts toward gossip, and you decide to apply what you have learned. You might say something like this: "You know, we have been friends for a long time and I really enjoy our talks together. But I have noticed that we have gotten into the habit of gossiping. This week, I've begun to memorize a verse related to that. [Share Ephesians 4:29 from memory.] The more I've thought about this verse, the more I have asked God to 'set a guard over my mouth . . . [and] keep watch over the door of my lips'[Psalm 141:3]. I now realize that I've been tearing you down rather than building you up by what I've said. Would you forgive me for that and join me in a project of speaking only wholesome words to one another?"

Now, your friend could be offended and might react to your statement, but I doubt it. He or she, too, may be convicted about his or her unwholesome speech and may want to share with you in this step of obedience.

The Wand or the Word

God's Word is not a magic wand we wave over our negative circumstances in order to see them transformed into a Cinderella experience. Rather, it is the powerful truth of a perfect God which, when applied to life, yields great blessing and benefit.

If you discovered gold, would you rebury it? If the doctor prescribed a life-saving medication, would you store it away and forget to take it? If God gave you a divine road map for living, would you just ignore it? Of course not!

God has given us something more precious than gold and more life-giving than the finest wonder drug. He has given us His Word. The only logical and sensible response we can give to His truth is to apply it. Won't you commit yourself to doing that in your life?

 Prayer

Father, thank You so much for Your life-giving and guiding Word. I want to be a doer of Your Word and not merely a hearer. But, it seems I have a tendency to listen and not act. Please help me, by Your power, to regularly apply what I am learning so that my life might mean something for Your glory. In Jesus' name, amen.

Part 3

The Practice of Renewing Your Mind

Who's Who in You?

In recent years there has been an increase in the number of *Who's Who* books that are being published. A book publishing company will pick a locality, determine who some of the better-known citizens are, and then offer them an opportunity to be in the *Who's Who of Crabtree Corners*. Being listed in this type of book, no matter what its origin, seems to signify that a person really is somebody.

Will the Real You Please Stand Up?

Why should people need to see their name in *Who's Who*? What benefit could there possibly be in this sort of recognition? Many would say that the benefit would be the improvement of a person's self-esteem. This idea of self-esteem has, in recent years, become one of the most talked-about issues in Christian and non-Christian circles alike.

One of the earlier writers on this subject said:

> The most important psychological discovery of this century is the discovery of the "self image." Whether we realize it or not, each of us carries about with us a mental blueprint or picture of

ourselves. It may be vague and ill-defined to our conscious gaze. In fact, it may not be consciously recognizable at all. But it is there, complete down to the last detail. This self image is our own conception of the "sort of person I am." It has been built up from our own beliefs about ourselves. But most of these beliefs about ourselves have unconsciously been formed from our past experiences, our successes and failures, our humiliations, our triumphs, and the way other people have reacted to us, especially in early childhood. From all these we mentally construct a "self"(or a picture of a self). Once an idea or a belief about ourselves goes into this picture, it becomes "true," as far as we personally are concerned. We do not question its validity, but proceed to act upon it just as if it were true.[1]

Maltz, quoted above, was somewhat of a pioneer in raising our awareness to this idea of how we view ourselves and its impact on our lives. Much of what he says has validity, but we must be very careful not to get caught up in the self-esteem movement without some careful discernment based upon God's Word.

While we want to be cautious about the perspectives of self-esteem proponents, it does appear that many people are seeking to be recognized as "somebody" by others because they are not convinced of their own value. If they were asked to tell someone who they really are, most likely they couldn't do so. They have all constructed a mental picture of what they are like based oftentimes upon misinformation. Comments and appraisals given to them by their family and friends have helped to develop this image from their earliest recollections. The person who first said someone's ears were too large or that he was a poor math student "helped" to construct that person's mental picture.

A while back I was working in the garage as my young son was playing nearby with his friends. He did something that I thought was very foolish. In my anger, I lashed out at him and said, "You were stupid to do that!" I immediately realized that I had embarrassed both him and his friends with my unkind and inaccurate statement. His action was indeed foolish, but *he* was not stupid. A biblical response to that situation would have been to take him aside privately and show him that his action was thoughtless and correction was necessary. What I had done, however, was to help program his self-image with inaccurate information. My son was not stupid, but he might well begin to believe that what I had said was factual and it would then become part of his own view of himself. My sinful reaction needed correction and my son deserved better. The occasion provided not only an opportunity for me to apologize to my son and his friends, but also to relay some correct information to him about himself and his value.

James Dobson reminds us,

> We are not what we think we are.
> We are not even what *others* think we are.
> We are what we *think* others think we are.[2]

Fuzzy Images

Supposed Superiority

Does the Bible have anything to say about your self-image? Consider for a moment a verse following a passage we studied earlier (Romans 12:1-2). It is very possible for you to have a distorted view of yourself because you have taken the world's opinion rather than God's Word as your measurement. Having emphasized the need for being "transformed by the renewing of your mind" (Romans 12:2), the writer now says, "Do not think of yourself more highly than you ought, but rather think of yourself with sober judgment, in accordance with the measure of faith God has given you" (Romans 12:3). If we are developing a new mind, we will also be developing a new self-image, one based upon God's correct *information*.

We are first challenged "not to think of yourself more highly than you ought." There is a definite play on words in this verse. Four times a form of the word *mind* is used in the original Greek text. Don't be "high-minded" beyond how you should "be minded," but "be minded" so as to be "sober minded." This repetition may seem a bit confusing, but certainly the apostle Paul had a Spirit-directed purpose for emphasizing the mind in this way. He has just told us that our minds must be "renewed." Now he says that if our minds are renewed, we will think in a new and accurate way about ourselves.

Some of us, unfortunately, are prideful, and we think of ourselves more highly than we should. The world certainly encourages this kind of thinking with its constant bombardment of "you are somebody special" messages. You, in fact, *are* special, but the question is, "Special compared to what?" How should we measure our self-worth?

In 1 Samuel 16, God told Samuel to anoint a new king He had chosen. As Samuel surveyed the sons of Jesse, he assumed that the most imposing of them, Eliab, must surely be the man. But God said, "Do not consider his appearance or his height, for I have rejected him. The LORD does not look at the things man looks at. Man looks at the outward appearance, but the LORD looks at the heart."[3] How often our image of ourselves or others is based upon a faulty measurement—that of physical beauty. God Himself is not above calling someone handsome or beautiful in His Word, but when He speaks of worth, He makes it very clear that it is an internal attribute of the heart.

Some people may go about with a "supposed superiority" because of their visible attributes or talents, and according to the world's viewpoint, they should "flaunt it if they've got it!" But God looks at character, not cosmetics.

It is interesting to realize that the Scriptures say very little about self-esteem, with the Romans passage being the central teaching. On the other hand, the matter of pride and its damaging effects comes up again and again. In both the Old and New Testaments, we are told God opposes the proud but gives grace to the humble.[4] We are then given this challenge: "Humble yourselves before the Lord, and he will lift you up" (James 4:10).

It seems quite clear that the greatest danger we face is not a low self-image, but rather a problem with pride. When Jesus speaks of the self, He never says we need to raise our self-esteem; rather, He states that we must deny ourselves and take up our cross and follow Him (see Mark 8:34).

Great care and conscientious biblical study is needed as we discuss the matter of self-esteem so that we do not turn a balanced appraisal of ourselves into an excuse for prideful living.

Supposed Inferiority

It is also possible to have an improper self-image of ourselves through a "supposed inferiority." Certainly if we are not to think more highly of ourselves than we ought, the converse is true. This kind of thinking is also faulty and may be just as damaging to a proper view of ourselves.

Dobson illustrates this well in his account about a young woman he calls Helen High School, who seems to have everything against her. From her earliest memory, she has seen herself as homely and hopeless. One day, after an especially hurtful experience, Helen fell on her bed in tears and pictured herself as standing before a judge and jury, on trial for being unacceptable in a world of beautiful people. The attorney for the prosecution pointed out how Helen, as far back as the fourth grade, was recognized as unworthy of recognition. On Valentine's Day, while her "beautiful" cousin was given 34 cards from love-sick boys, Helen received only three— "two from girls and one from her Uncle Albert in San Antonio."[5] Illustration after illustration was brought to prove that Helen had absolutely nothing to offer the world. The jury, made up of only "beautiful" and "intelligent" people, found her guilty and the judge sentenced her with these words:

> Helen High School, a jury of your peers has found you to be unacceptable to the human race. You are hereby sentenced to a life of loneliness. You will probably fail in everything you do, and you'll go to your grave without a friend in the world. Marriage is out of the question, and there will never be a child in your home. You are a failure, Helen. You're a disappointment to your parents and must be considered excess baggage from this point forward. This case is hereby closed.[6]

Sadly enough, Helen's appraisal of herself is shared by many Christians who have formed an image of themselves based upon false information. In a gathering of believers, one will regularly hear people speaking of their supposed deficiencies. When challenged to point out the "real" Christians among them, many disqualify themselves and speak of the Miss America runner-up who sang last Sunday night or the six-foot-nine-inch basketball star who can "stuff" a basketball but can't quote John 3:16.

Paul strongly exhorts that we are to think of ourselves with sober judgment (Romans 12:3). The original word for "sober" actually means "to be in your right mind"! If you think more highly of yourself than you ought or if you live with a supposed inferiority, you're not in your right mind.

Comparing Apples with Oranges

"But how," you may ask, "do I clear up my thinking about myself?" You must begin by making proper comparisons. Paul chides the Corinthians for "measur[ing] themselves by themselves and compar[ing] themselves with themselves" (2 Corinthians 10:12). He considers them lacking in understanding. In order to have a proper self-image, we must measure ourselves with the proper yardstick. Romans 12:3 says we are to think about ourselves "in accordance with the measure [allotment] of faith God has given you." The measurement is God's allotment, not man's assessment. The issue is not how I compare with someone else, but rather, how I am living in obedience to Christ and using the abilities He has given me for His glory. We read in Galatians 6:3-5, "If anyone thinks he is something when he is nothing, he deceives himself. Each one should test his own actions. Then he can take pride in himself, without comparing himself to someone else, for each one should carry his own load."

One-of-a-Kind

You alone are you! God has designed and equipped you in a unique way not exactly matched by any other person. The example of spiritual gifts is used as an illustration in the verses that follow Romans 12:3. We are unified as "one body with many members," yet we are also diverse: "these members do not all have the same function" (verses 4-6). Twenty people in your church may be gifted as teachers (verse 7), but no two of them will teach exactly the same way. Why? Because along with that Spirit-given enablement, God has given certain talents and attributes that will be used as a platform for the exercise of the gift.

The promise of Romans 12:3 is that *every* believer has been given this "measure of faith." No one is left out. Not even you! When you are looking at yourself and determining your value, it would be foolish to see yourself as you believe others see you. You must first and foremost recognize how *God* sees you! Your assessment must be based upon God's information if it is to be realistic.

God's Glasses

People are sometimes accused of looking at the world through rose-colored glasses. As Christians, we should be looking at both ourselves and our world through God's glasses. How He sees us should determine how we see ourselves.

Let's be practical and apply some of the principles of a renewed mind to this topic of self-esteem. How can we begin to see ourselves in a new and healthy way? The truth which we discovered in chapter four is foundational to an accurate self-esteem: If you have crossed that bridge of choice which we mentioned, deciding not to be conformed but to be transformed, then the following steps will lead you to a balanced view of yourself.

1. *Carefully examine your present self-image.* Be honest with yourself. How do you really view yourself? Is there either a supposed superiority or

inferiority? Is your self-concept based upon biblical truth, or upon years of misinformation from others?

If you are not sure that you can properly analyze your own self-image, you may want to ask one or two trusted Christian friends to help you evaluate yourself. Be careful that you ask friends who love you enough to be objective, honest, and constructive and who will evaluate you with a biblical perspective.

2. *Learn as much about yourself as you can from God's Word.* What does He say about your position before Him in Christ? Don Matzat, in his very helpful book *Christ Esteem*, discusses the importance of looking for your worth and your happiness in the right place. If you focus on yourself, you will find only frustration and disappointment. If, however, you look at Christ, the result will be very different. He says:

> When you look at yourself, you must see your sin. When you look away from yourself unto Christ Jesus, you see your new identity, your perfect righteousness, your glorious position with God in the heavenly places. Your life in this world, your peace, your joy and contentment is not dependent upon "how" you look. It depends upon "where" you look.[7]

By looking at Christ and His Word, you will bring your view of yourself into clearer focus. How does He view your spiritual giftedness and abilities? What does He have to say about the potential of your life and His willingness to effectively use you in significant ways?

You may find yourself, as did the spies of Moses' time, in the midst of a disagreement (Numbers 13:17-33). Ten of them looked over the Promised Land and saw it as impregnable. They said the land was inhabited by giants and "we seemed like grasshoppers *in our own eyes*, and we looked the same to them" (verse 33, emphasis added). These ten *saw themselves* as they believed the enemy in the land viewed them. But you will remember that the two remaining spies, Joshua and Caleb, differed with them. Caleb reported, "We should go up and take possession of the land, for we can certainly do it" (verse 30). These two men realized that God is always a majority! They viewed themselves as able to conquer because they saw themselves through God's eyes. A proper self-image is impossible apart from the correct information about you, which is found only in God's Word.

3. *Reorganize your personal priorities.* You may well be putting your energies into the wrong solution to your esteem problem.

There is a tremendous emphasis upon the body in our society today. Many of the television commercials that we see day after day tell us how to please, pamper, empower, and pump up our bodies. We are told that if we improve our looks with a certain diet or exercise program, or if we cover our bodies with more attractive cosmetics or clothing, we will feel better about ourselves.

The clear message is "change your body, and you will change your image." There is little doubt that having a good physical appearance can have a positive effect on your self-concept, but that's merely a surface change that does little to change what we really are as a person. Paul says to Timothy, "Physical training is of some value, but godliness has value for all things, holding promise for both the present life and the life to come" (1 Timothy 4:8).

Our emphasis needs to be on the development of character, not on the reconstruction of our bodies. You cannot become Christlike by submitting to the knife of the plastic surgeon. The image that we are to be conformed to is not related to the physical aspect of our lives, but to the spiritual.[8]

We need only to look back into our high-school yearbooks to see that those who were described as "most likely to fail" became in many cases the truly successful people of today. Why? Because they were developing their character while others were busy combing their hair.

4. *Discover your spiritual gift.* As we saw earlier, God has gifted each believer, and it is part of the raw material which is used to build a proper self-image. Our self-worth will be directly linked to how we "produce" for God. If we recognize that our labors for the Lord will produce fruit that is lasting, we will feel better about ourselves. At the same time, keep in mind that your worth to God is always great no matter where you are in your spiritual productivity.

As you discover and use your spiritual gift, you will sense the power of the Spirit working through you as will the people around you.

5. *Build up one another.* We all need to realize how we affect one another's self-esteem. As believers

in Jesus Christ, we are "individually members one of another" (Romans 12:5 NASB). Our spiritual gifts are given to build up the body.[9]

Each of us will have a great deal to do with how other believers view themselves and therefore how effectively they will be able to serve God. Some Christians seem to see themselves as a committee of one appointed to reveal the weaknesses and sins of all those around them. The Scripture, however, views this as the opposite of our purpose. "Therefore encourage one another and build each other up, just as in fact you are doing" (1 Thessalonians 5:11). You and I can be greatly used of God in helping others to recognize their God-given potential and purpose.

An even stronger challenge is found in Philippians 2:1-5, where Paul describes the mind and attitude of Christ. He says that like Jesus we should:

> Do nothing out of selfish ambition or vain conceit, but in humility consider [esteem] others better than yourselves. Each of you should look not only to your own interests, but also to the interests of others (verses 3-4).

It is a powerful encouragement to us to realize that God is willing to use us in ways that benefit the lives of our fellow believers.

The Image Maker

Why not begin to apply the principles we have just examined? Look at your self-image in light of God's *information*. *Memorize* and *meditate* upon His truth as it relates to the real you. *Imagine* yourself not according to the faulty picture that has been developed through years of improper input, but on the basis of the truth. And *apply* what you are learning to your experience, immediately allowing the principles of the Word to become the practice of your life.

As your mind is renewed, your life will be transformed ... and that transformation will first be seen as you begin to get a proper view of the new you!

Prayer

Dear Lord, thank You for the way You have designed me. Help me, through the eyes of Your Word, to see myself as I really am and then, by Your grace, to become the person You desire me to be. In Jesus' name, amen.

"It Is Written"

It was almost as if the car was steering itself. He had driven down this dark street before and had determined many times never to choose this route again. The reason? This street led to a very seedy section of town where a number of all-night strip joints were located. For as long as he could remember, the temptation that was most overpowering to him was sexual lust. He could never admit it to those he loved most because he was afraid they would not understand. He already hated himself for the thoughts that regularly ran through his mind and seemed to drive him now toward his destination. He couldn't bear the thought of the people he cared about hating him as well, and being embarrassed by his lack of self-control. It seemed so strange that he was even headed down this street tonight. Only a few days before, he and his wife, whom he adored, had celebrated their tenth anniversary. Not two days later, he had received a commendation from his boss with a raise included. God had blessed him so much.

But, the battle raged in his mind as the car continued toward his rendezvous with the sin that both enticed and energized him even while, at the same moment, making him physically ill. Why couldn't he be like some men he knew who seemed so in control of themselves? Or were they just like him, hiding their own sin while putting on a front?

He had been a believer long enough that this old tape of his former life should have been erased by now. There were good days when his mind stayed pure, but then the urges would again overwhelm him and he would find himself, almost as if it were not really him, driving down this street once again. Only a few blocks remained between him and the sin which would riddle him with guilt once more. "God, help me!" He prayed. "Please don't let me fail again!" He heard himself praying out loud, but was anyone listening? He felt so very tired as he drove on.

A Common Problem

Everyone struggles with temptation of one sort or another. God says it is common to us all.[1]

Perhaps you are struggling with a physical addiction to alcohol or you are regularly overwhelmed with anger or anxiety. Maybe the sin that regularly entangles you has to do with gambling, overeating, overspending, or talking improperly to those you love. Or possibly you struggle with lust, as did the man we just read about and will meet again later. Whatever your struggle may be, the renewing of your mind will have a tremendous impact on your life in the area of overcoming temptation.

In Hebrews 4:14-16, we are challenged with these words:

> Since we have a great high priest who has gone through the heavens, Jesus the Son of God, let us hold firmly to the faith we profess. For we do not have a high priest who is unable to sympathize with our weaknesses, but we have one who has

been tempted in every way, just as we are—yet was without sin. Let us then approach the throne of grace with confidence, so that we may receive mercy and find grace to help us in our time of need.

This passage of Scripture offers us great encouragement by reminding us that the many types of temptations we face daily were experienced by Jesus as well. But oftentimes we live as if these verses were not really true. We do not identify with the songwriter who wrote, "God said it, I believe it, and that settles it for me." Rather, we are more apt to think, "God said it, I believe it, but it doesn't apply to me!" We will admit that Jesus was "tempted in every way," but then we are quick to add, "He is God, so the temptation wasn't the same. He couldn't sin, but I can and I do!"

In our desire to overcome our struggles, we most likely have come across 1 Corinthians 10:13, where we read, "No temptation has seized you except what is common to man. And God is faithful; he will not let you be tempted beyond what you can bear. But when you are tempted, he will also provide a way out so that you can stand up under it." In response we might find ourselves saying, "I want to believe and apply these verses to my life, Lord, but somehow their truth is beyond me."

How can we bring our lives into alignment with these principles of Scripture? How can we come before the "throne of grace" and find help in our "time of need"?

Believing that the Word of God is true when it states that Jesus "has been tempted . . . as we are" and that God does "provide a way out," let's look at the historical record of Jesus' temptation in the wilderness as found in Luke chapter 4. These verses are *information* with which we can begin to renew our minds so that we can know victory over temptation.

For the next few moments, read *slowly* and *carefully* Luke 4:1-13:

> Jesus, full of the Holy Spirit, returned from the Jordan and was led by the Spirit in the desert, where for forty days he was tempted by the devil. He ate nothing during those days, and at the end of them he was hungry.
>
> The devil said to him, "If you are the Son of God, tell this stone to become bread."
>
> Jesus answered, "It is written: 'Man does not live on bread alone.'"
>
> The devil led him up to a high place and showed him in an instant all the kingdoms of the world. And he said to him, "I will give you all their authority and splendor, for it has been given to me, and I can give it to anyone I want to. So if you worship me, it will all be yours."
>
> Jesus answered, "It is written: 'Worship the Lord your God and serve him only.'"
>
> The devil led him to Jerusalem and had him stand on the highest point of the temple. "If you are the Son of God," he said, "throw yourself down from here. For it is written: 'He will command his angels concerning you to guard you carefully; they will lift you up in their hands, so that you will not strike your foot against a stone.'"
>
> Jesus answered, "It says, 'Do not put the Lord your God to the test.'"
>
> When the devil had finished all this tempting, he left him until an opportune time.

Someone has categorized Jesus' three temptations as appetite, avarice, and ambition. I believe these three words will help us understand how Jesus was tempted "as we are" and His response to the temptations will explain why He "yet was without sin." (A similar discussion of these three types of temptation is found in 1 John 2:15-17, a passage you may find helpful.) Keep in mind that although Jesus was tempted "in every way," that doesn't mean He received every individual temptation possible, but that He was tempted in the same three *categories* of temptation that Satan has used on all of us since the beginning of time in the Garden of Eden.[2]

What We Need to Know About Temptation

In Jesus' encounter with Satan as described by Luke, we see several important principles about dealing with temptation. Let's look at them together.

When We're Most Vulnerable

Mountaintop Experiences

The previous chapter of Luke tells of a very vivid experience in Jesus' life, His baptism. This event signaled the beginning of His ministry and was accompanied by a miraculous opening of the heavens, the visible descent of the Holy Spirit, and an audible word from God, in which He commended His Son (Luke 3:21-22).

In our present day, we might define this event as a "mountaintop experience." It was an emotional and spiritual high point in Christ's earthly life. It is not surprising then, that Satan immediately tried to tempt Jesus. The principle here is this: *We are more susceptible to temptation following a mountaintop experience.* When our emotions have been stretched to new heights, we are vulnerable to descending to new depths if we are not on guard. Our emotional system seems to respond that way.

We cannot maintain a high emotional pitch for a pro-
longed period without placing ourselves in a position of
vulnerability. Now, that doesn't mean there is anything
wrong with emotionally charged situations—especially
if they are in response to a step of obedience as was
Christ's baptism. However, we need to realize that we
may be more susceptible to temptation following such
an experience.

Moments of Weakness

Luke 4 also notes that Jesus was led about in the
wilderness for 40 days without food. We are told, "He ate
nothing during those days" (verse 2). It is not surprising,
then, that Satan's first temptation played upon Christ's
physical hunger and weakness. This brings us to our
second principle: *We are more susceptible to temptation
when in poor physical condition.*

You might respond by saying, "Well, I knew that." But
let me ask you: When you were last tempted, did you
give any thought to your physical health? Is it possible
that you were tired, hungry, or even ill? Being physically
run down is not a valid excuse for sinning, but it is an
"early warning" device for your possible susceptibility.

Satan's temptation to Jesus was in the area of
appetite. He said to Christ, "If you are the Son of God,
tell this stone to become bread" (Luke 4:3). This challenge to appetite, of course, isn't limited to the stomach.
We all have other passions that cry out for fulfillment.
Webster defines appetite as "an inherent, habitual desire
for some personal gratification."

Now, appetite is certainly not all bad. Without it, we
would starve to death. Many of our appetites are honorable when kept in balance. The person who overeats
is no more or less out of control than the person who is
controlled by some lust or selfish desire. We all crave

satisfaction in this area, but temptation becomes sin when we yield to an improper solution for our hunger.

Our Source of Power

We would do well here to consider another important principle and, at the same time, solve a problem discussed earlier in this chapter. The principle is this: *The Holy Spirit supplies the power to resist temptation.*

According to Luke 4:1, Jesus was "full of the Holy Spirit." The Greek word for "full" is also used in Ephesians 5:18, where we as believers are told to be "filled with the Spirit." This raises a very important point: When Jesus resisted temptation, He did so in the same way that we are to resist temptation—in the power of the Spirit.

Some people say that Christ, though He was tempted, cannot really relate to our struggles because He is God and therefore He couldn't sin. That, however, is not true. Here's a simple illustration that might help to put this in perspective: Many homes have both a solid front door and a screen door. In good weather, we open the main door and allow the fresh air, not the bugs, to come through the screen door. Now, picture the front door as Christ's Godhood and the bugs as temptation. If the screen door were left open and the bugs got through, they could never penetrate the solid front door. In other words, if temptation got as far as Christ's Godhood, He couldn't sin because He is God. However, as seen in Luke 4, temptation never reached the closed, solid front door. It was first repelled by the screen door, which is the Holy Spirit. The exciting truth here is that Christ did not resist temptation because He was God, but because He was controlled by the Holy Spirit. He resisted in the same power that is available to every believer—the Holy Spirit.

Christ was tempted just like we are, and He resisted just as we can, too, if we are "full of the Holy Spirit."

Satan's Desire to Control

The next temptation Satan presented to Christ is that of *avarice*. Avarice is defined as "an inordinate desire for wealth or greed for things."

Somehow Satan led Christ to a place where He could view all the kingdoms of the world, which emphasizes our next principle: *Satan is the god of this world and will promise much to control us.* As the god of this world,[3] the devil will use the enticement of things to gain a foothold in our lives. He will promise us much in order to turn our worship away from God. We need only look at the grip that materialism has on many of us to recognize how effective Satan has been. "I would never worship Satan," you might retort. I'm sure you wouldn't, but how often has the thought of a new car, house, or some other material possession become an obsession to the point of distracting you from "pure devotion to Christ"?[4]

A number of years ago, I became possessed with the idea of owning a motor home. I was able to rationalize my desire well and could easily find a dozen good "spiritual" reasons why my family and I needed this home on wheels. For a number of weeks, I hardly thought of anything else; and I must admit, my relationship with the Lord was somewhere in the background of my life during that period. When the time finally came and I owned that vehicle (it was an antiquated model), I was certain I would be happy. You know what happened, don't you? I found my avarice wasn't satisfied even when the coveted item was in my possession. The crafty god of this world deceived me into believing I could satisfy spiritual anemia with a material transfusion. It will never work; therefore, Jesus gave us a clear example as to how we should respond to Satan's offer.

The Power of Scripture

Jesus responded to the second temptation by repeating, "It is written" (Luke 4:8). He then quoted Scripture in answer to Satan's ploy. That brings us to our next principle: *We must use Scripture to resist temptation.*

We are not told that Jesus carried the Old Testament scrolls with Him, so we must assume He had the Scriptures memorized. I believe we can also expect that He meditated and prepared Himself ahead of time for temptation.

Preventative Maintenance

During my time in the Army, I learned a procedure called "preventative maintenance." This process was a bit overdone on the base where I was stationed, for I remember painting the same five-ton truck three times before it was driven even once. The idea of preventative maintenance, however, is sound and applicable to dealing with temptation. Once we are in the midst of a tempting situation, it is probably too late to look for a way of escape. But if we consider our weaknesses and do some preventative maintenance ahead of time, we will be ready. That preparation will include the discovery of Scripture passages that speak directly to our needs and weaknesses. We must then memorize them, meditate upon them, and imagine ourselves in the midst of temptation responding in a biblical manner. Then when the temptation overtakes us, we will be ready to say, "It is written."

Escape Routes

The first time I traveled across a mountain range, I was surprised to see short dead-end roads every few miles on the downhill side of the highway. It was not until I saw a sign explaining the purpose of these roads that I realized they were specially prepared safety exits for runaway trucks with brakes that had failed. These short dead-end roads were covered with lots of sand, which would help to slow down out-of-control trucks that had exited onto one of these spurs.

When we suddenly find ourselves on a downhill run without our brakes, heading for sin, we, too, need a previously prepared emergency road we can take to stop our momentum. The Word of God, if it is a part of our hearts and minds, will provide that "escape route" when needed.

The Danger of Wrong Ambition

The third temptation Satan offered to Christ was *ambition*. Webster says ambition is "an eager or inordinate desire for preferment, for honor, superiority, power and attainment." Satan took Christ to Jerusalem and set Him on the pinnacle of the temple, probably some 150 feet above the ground. The deceiver then quoted Scripture to Christ in an effort to convince Jesus to jump and trust God to save Him from death.[5] The temptation of ambition was valid, for if Christ had jumped and been saved, all of those who witnessed this spectacle would certainly have proclaimed Him to be miraculous and elevated Him to a place of prominence long before God's appointed time.

Don't put it past Satan to misuse Scripture in his attempt to deceive. Many of the cults today are formed around the misinterpretation or misapplication of God's

Word. Satan is not above using any means to accomplish his devious purposes.

Our next principle is this: *You and I will also be offered temptations that stimulate our desire to "be somebody" and to have position and prestige.* Now, I might add that ambition in itself is not wrong. Without it, you would not get out of bed in the morning or eagerly seek to accomplish any worthwhile purpose. Ambition becomes a problem only when we step outside of the bounds of Scripture to fulfill our desire.

Jesus recognized Satan's temptation for what it was and, in the power of the Spirit, answered with Scripture. "It is said, you shall not put the Lord your God to the test" (Luke 4:12 NASB; see Deuteronomy 6:16). When we reach out to accomplish our own ambitious purposes for personal advancement, we are putting God to the test. We are stepping outside of His prescribed boundaries and then asking for His help to preserve us from harm. It is like driving off a cliff and then rolling down the window to cry out for God to save you. Or, in an example more of us can relate to, we test God when we buy something for $20,000 to keep up with the Joneses and then ask God to help us pay the monthly payments, which are beyond us. When we plan our lives with little consideration for the principles God has given and then ask Him to bail us out of the consequences of our ambitions, we are putting Him to the test.

How We Can Have Victory

Christ's example is applicable to your life and mine. The three categories of temptation presented to Him are the same that we will face. And the principles we learned from looking at Christ's response to temptation are guidelines we can use to help us successfully resist the temptations we encounter today.

We have by no means exhausted all of the helpful principles found in Luke 4; for example, there is another one in verse 13: "When the devil had finished all this tempting, he left [Jesus] until an opportune time." Simply stated, *Satan will not give up easily*. In other words, you will continue to be bombarded with temptation; yet, you can still be a victor. If you follow Christ's example as found in Luke chapter 4 and discover the many existing principles in God's Word that relate to dealing with temptation, you will be able to "resist the devil"[6] as did Jesus.

As you renew your mind through the biblical process we have outlined, you will begin to sense a new strength. Why not choose one area of your life right now that has often been a source of disappointment and failure? Search the Scriptures to discover specific principles that counteract this "sin that so easily entangles"[7] you. Memorize and meditate upon the truths that apply and then imagine yourself a victor as you prepare yourself for the temptation.

The Way of Escape

As the man drove down the dark street, coming closer to fulfilling his temptation, it seemed as if someone was speaking to him. The words slowly but surely came to his mind:

> It is God's will that you should be sanctified: that you should avoid sexual immorality; that each of you should learn to control his own body in a way that is holy and honorable, not in passionate lust like the heathen, who do not know God.[8]

"Is that You talking, God?" Those were the verses he had memorized three weeks before because he wanted to hide God's Word in his heart to keep him from slipping into sin again. The voice, or whatever it was, continued:

> No temptation has seized you except what is common to man. And God is faithful; he will not let you be tempted beyond what you can bear. But when you are tempted, he will also provide a way out so that you can stand up under it.[9]

A way out? An escape route? What was it? With all of the powerful desires that had carried him along during the last few moments, he had almost forgotten the guideline he had recently learned. He realized that earlier in the day, when he first recognized his thoughts for what they were, he should have taken them captive—but he allowed them to remain. Now he understood the need to capture his thoughts and bring them into obedience to Christ—the need to *refuse* the tempting thoughts and *replace* them with God's pure word. Suddenly, other verses came to mind that he had memorized only a few days before, including 1 Thessalonians 4:7-8:

> God did not call us to be impure, but to live a holy life. Therefore, he who rejects this instruction does not reject man but God, who gives you his Holy Spirit.

"Oh, Lord, I don't want to reject You! You say You have given me Your Holy Spirit. I need His help right now!"

As the man spoke these words, his foot moved to the brake and he pulled to the side of the street. He quickly locked the doors and looked down the street where, not two blocks away, the bright lights flashed their impure invitation to him.

"Lord, I don't want to disappoint You again. I hate the sin that has ravaged my soul over and over. I ask You to help me take Your way of escape right now. Please empower me to choose Your way of purity instead of Satan's deceptive plan, which leads to destruction."

He looked one more time at the brightly colored signs beckoning him. He took a deep breath, lifted his foot off the brake, and began to move slowly down the street again. As he reached an intersection, he whispered one more brief prayer: "Help me, Lord!" With that prayer, he turned the wheel and drove around the corner onto a side street. He then stepped on the accelerator and headed toward the freeway. As he turned onto the freeway onramp, he suddenly began to feel a weight lifting off of him. The lust that had been so strong only a few minutes before faded in significance. As he assumed freeway speed and merged into traffic, a sense of peace and hope swept over him. "Thank You, Lord, for showing me how faithful You are!" He now looked forward to arriving home to the family he loved so much!

Prayer

Thank You, Father, for the example Christ set. I pray that You will fill me with Your Spirit and empower me to resist the devil. Help me, Lord, to discover the Scriptures that apply to my situation and to use them to aid me in experiencing victory for Your glory. In Jesus' name, amen.

Coping with Constant Confusion

In the early 1950s, R.G. LeTourneau and three other men were flying in a small plane near the Andes Mountains. The size of the men and comparative power of the plane were not matched; therefore, shortly after takeoff, the plane faltered and plunged into a raging jungle river. As it hit the water, it flipped upside down and began to sink. All four men were able to get out of the plane but found themselves in a life-and-death struggle with the violently swirling river. After a number of exhausting minutes during which they attempted to overcome the strong current to reach the shore, one of the weakened men gave up and slipped under the water. Much to his surprise, only 30 inches beneath the surface, his feet struck bottom. Immediately, he stood up and called for his friends to stop struggling and stand up. Somewhat embarrassed but certainly relieved, all four men walked to the safety of the riverbank.

This true story has a direct application to the stressful lives in which we exist. Many of us are worn almost to exhaustion in our struggle against the currents of life for we, also, have not realized there is a way to stand up and walk out.

A mind being renewed by God's Word will be able to see life differently. What one person would define as unbearable stress, another with a new mind will see as an opportunity to trust in an all-sufficient God.

The Good Old Days

If you are like me you have probably wondered what it would have been like to live 100 years ago. Most likely you've imagined a small, quiet town where a traffic jam is nothing more than two horse-drawn carriages entering Main Street at the same time. The town square is peaceful as a few people walk quietly by and even the children call out to each other in their playtime with muffled voices. Shopping is an enjoyable pastime and the peak of excitement is a leisurely Sunday-school picnic on a Saturday afternoon.

However, history gives us a different picture. The Civil War was still on everyone's mind with all its terrifying agonies. Race relations and rampant crime were a daily tension. Oh, it's true that the pace was slower and the environment quieter, but the average individual who lived 100 years ago also had to cope with many different stresses related to that time. Merely surviving was a much more time-consuming task than it is today with all our modern conveniences.

If we want to trace man's tensions even farther back, we need only to read the book of Job. One of the oldest recorded histories, Job's life was anything but an example of peace and tranquility. From the position of a wealthy landowner Job was quickly transported to a terrible existence. We find Job in chapter 2 with all his cattle and sheep gone, his servants dead, and his children laying lifeless beneath a collapsed house. Then, we see Job sitting on a dung hill covered with boils, and his wife screaming, "Why don't you curse God and die?" As if all that weren't enough, three purported friends come on the scene to "comfort" Job by condemning him for his supposed sinfulness. Now that is stress!

As we can see, the good old days were not much different from our present days when it comes to stressful circumstances. Pressures, tensions, and confusion have always been a part of life.

What Is Stress?

Gary Collins wrote:

> The word "stress" was first used in physics and engineering. It referred to the severe forces that might be put on a building or bridge. It is this kind of stress which sometimes causes buildings to collapse because of the weight of ice or the power of a violent wind. Later, the term "stress" was taken over by medicine, physiology, economics, sociology and other fields of science; but for most people, the word has come to have a distinctly psychological meaning. There have been many scholarly attempts to define psychological stress, but one of the best and most down-to-earth definitions came several years ago from a biologist named Hans Selve. "Stress," he said, "is essentially the wear and tear of living." Aaron Beck adds some insight when he says stress is "a force of sufficient magnitude to distort or deform when applied to a system." We must recognize that stressful situations are not only those of great proportions. Often it is not the major catastrophe that crushes us but the combination of "minor" tensions from improperly squeezed toothpaste tubes to dripping

> faucets. These kinds of stresses mount and build
> until the sum of their parts is absolutely over-
> powering and our system short-circuits.[1]

Interestingly enough, what may be stressful for one person may have little affect on another. One individual may be totally frustrated by a barking dog in an otherwise quiet neighborhood, while another loves all of the noises and confusion of city life. At times, we seem to have contradictory responses in our own lives. We may feel constant tension because our home is too small, but find a week of camping in a tent relaxing. You and I must define as stressful those things which bring us to our knees whether or not our friends would consider them a problem.

A Remedy for Stress

Does the Bible deal with the matter of stress? Yes, it certainly does, and in a clear, concise way that can ultimately help us to cope with *any* situation if we are willing to apply its principles. One extremely helpful passage is found in Philippians 4:4-13; here, the apostle Paul deals with difficult situations and gives clear biblical answers to coping with life as it really is.

Rejoicing in the Lord

Paul's first statements, rather than demonstrating how to cope, explain what life will be like when we are coping. An illustration or two will help us here: Diet plans are sold by picturing the *before* and the *after*. Bald-headed men are enticed to buy a toupee by viewing the handsome results of a full crop of hair on a previously sparse head. In a similar but serious way, the apostle explains how we will look if we are coping with life biblically: "Rejoice in the Lord always. I will say it again:

Rejoice! Let your gentleness be evident to all. The Lord is near" (Philippians 4:4-5). In these verses we see that there are two relationships that reveal the soundness of our response to the tensions of daily living. The first is our relationship with God; the second is our relationships with other people. Paul first comments on our relationship with God, saying that we are told to "rejoice *in the Lord*." To make the command even more emphatic, Paul says we are to "rejoice in the Lord *always*." Now we might think that occasional rejoicing is manageable, but that rejoicing *always* is too much! No one can ever do that! Right?

But, would God command us to do something that was impossible? Certainly not! Often we do not rejoice because we let our joy depend upon our *circumstances*. But Paul doesn't say to rejoice in your circumstances; he says, "Rejoice in the *Lord*." He wants us to have a joy that is dependent upon a consistent relationship with an unchanging God in the midst of a confused and changing world. The renewed mind will recognize that circumstances, no matter how negative, are opportunities to refocus on God and rejoice. Lest we miss Paul's challenge, he adds, "I will say it again: Rejoice!" (Philippians 4:4). Undoubtedly Paul's command confirms that it really is possible for us to know rejoicing at all times— even in the stressful moments in our life.

A few years ago, I had an errand to do in the center of town. I was on a tight schedule, so I brought along books I was studying on the subject of stress and set them on the front car seat. As I headed toward my destination, the clock seemed to race, but the traffic crawled. I became more and more tense as I realized the time of my appointment was fast approaching. After a number of miles of bumper-to-bumper frustration, I saw a space in the lane to the left and darted nervously out around the car ahead. Just as I made that move, I saw that someone else had a similar plan and he pulled right in front of me. At that moment, all my circuits shorted and I stomped on the brakes and came to a screeching halt inches from the car in front of me. As I stopped, one of the books on the seat tumbled to the floor and my eyes quickly scanned the title: *You Can Profit from Stress.* Momentarily, I went limp as I realized the very subject I was studying had just taken its toll on me. God used the title of that book to remind me I was not rejoicing in the Lord, but rather reeling from my circumstances.

Exhibiting Patience

Philippians 4:5 clearly mentions another relationship which demonstrates whether or not you are coping with stress "God's way." It says, "Let your gentleness be evident to all. The Lord is near." If we are properly dealing with our own tensions, we will be able to relate to others around us with a gentle patience.

Those who study behavior tell us that under stress, even the nicest of people tend to become aggressive and easily angered. This could explain the Dr. Jekyll-and-Mr. Hyde personalities on the freeway and the trampling mobs at rock concerts.

But Paul explains that those who are meeting life head-on with God's principles will have both their relationships with God and with those around them in balance.

Being Anxious for Nothing

The well-known words in Philippians 4:6 explain how we can cope with less-than-pleasant circumstances: "Do not be anxious about anything, but in everything, by prayer and petition, with thanksgiving, present your requests to God."

Anxiety is said to be present in epidemic proportions in our world today. Anxiety is what I experienced as I gripped the wheel of my car in frustration that afternoon when the book tumbled from the car seat. I was lacking God's peace; I hadn't even brought God in on my traffic problem or crowded schedule. I had not let my requests be made known to Him.

We are challenged here to "not be anxious about anything." Now, in the Greek text, that literally means *not anything*! There are no circumstances that can overpower God. That is why He tells us to come before Him in prayer; He wants us to tap into His power source.

Expressing Thanks to God

There are two important words in Philippians 4:6 that are often overlooked. Paul tells us in every situation to make our requests known "*with thanksgiving*." It is never easy to be thankful for tense, trying circumstances, but the injunction is clear. Whatever our feelings may be, we are to activate our will and "give thanks in all circumstances, for this is God's will for you in Christ Jesus" (1 Thessalonians 5:18). When we give thanks, we are showing that we really trust our sovereign God to do what is right in our life.

No matter how large or small your frustrations may be, you bring God's power to bear upon them when you make your requests known to Him. Obedience to this principle is like removing the valve on a pressure cooker and letting the excess steam escape.

Receiving God's Peace

Just the reading of Philippians 4:7 alone has a tremendously calming effect: "And the peace of God, which transcends all understanding, will guard your hearts and your minds in Christ Jesus." God's promise is that no matter how stressful your situation is, His peace is sufficient. What's more, this peace is beyond our understanding. It is far better than being beamed back 100 years to a quiet country town. It doesn't even require that you be released from the situation that is causing the tension. Rather, God's peace stands as a sentry at the gate of your heart and mind in the midst of stress.

Thinking Right Thoughts

Let's look briefly at the next verse, Philippians 4:8, which we will study more closely in the next chapter: "Finally, brothers, whatever is true, whatever is noble, whatever is right, whatever is pure, whatever is lovely, whatever is admirable—if anything is excellent or praiseworthy—think about such things."

We are again back to the very heart of what's involved in renewing the mind. The principle that makes it possible to cope with the tensions of life is this: *Let your mind dwell on God's thoughts!* Isaiah referred to this very principle when he said, "[God] will keep in perfect peace him whose mind [imagination] is steadfast, because he trusts in you" (Isaiah 26:3). Simply stated, Philippians 4:8-9 teach that if we consistently think about the right *information, meditate* (dwell) upon it, and put it into *practice,* we will be able to benefit from our stress. Paul then says, "Whatever you have learned or received or heard from me, or seen in me—put it into practice. And the God of peace will be with you" (Philippians 4:9).

Paul's Example of Contentment

Paul doesn't leave us wondering what these principles would look like in real life. He demonstrates from his own experience how he coped with stress:

> I am not saying this because I am in need, for I have learned to be content whatever the circumstances. I know what it is to be in need, and I know what it is to have plenty. I have learned the secret of being content in any and every situation, whether well fed or hungry, whether living in plenty or in want. I can do everything through him who gives me strength (Philippians 4:11-13).

Paul's example is most encouraging as we realize that his experience can be ours. He doesn't say that he went forward at a meeting and was zapped by some supernatural power, never to collapse under stress again. He didn't discover an instant solution to stress. No, in fact, he says he "learned" to cope in every circumstance. That he *learned* to cope indicates a process where he progressively came to a certain point in his knowledge and growth. Evidently, Paul met his circumstances whether shipwrecked (2 Corinthians 11:25) or imprisoned (2 Corinthians 6:5) by using the very principles taught to the Philippians.

Paul "learned to be content" not by changing his frustrating circumstances but by responding to them with the strength found in Christ (see Philippians 4:13). That strength was derived from focusing his mind on the things "worthy of praise"[2] rather than dwelling on the stressful situations of his life.

Put Your Feet Down

Is it possible that at this time, you are like R. G. LeTourneau and his friends who were struggling against the violent currents in their efforts to reach the riverbank? If you feel as if you are about to be pulled under, there is only one solution: Put your feet down. The solid footing of God's Word is there, just inches away.

Take Philippians 4:4-8 and apply these verses to your situation according to the suggestions given in chapters five through nine of this book—apply them in terms of information, memorization, meditation, imagination, and application. By putting Philippians 4:4-8 to work in your life, you'll see that it really *is* possible to think in new ways about the anxiety and stress in your life and find true peace and contentment.

Prayer

Lord, I have been knocked down time and again by my circumstances. I want to be able to cope with life Your way. Help me to apply Your wonderful principles to my life today and to experience Your peace as a result of obedience to Your Word. Thank You, Father, for giving me stressful situations so I can learn to depend upon You. In Jesus' name, amen.

Looking Ahead

Being a participant in a graduation ceremony has been a privilege for me on a number of different occasions; however, one of those times stands out in my mind. I remember it not because of the degree conferred, although I felt a great sense of accomplishment and relief when I was handed my diploma; rather, because of a simple mistake made by one of my fellow graduates, which still brings me a smile when I think about it. My class was the first to graduate in the new chapel on our seminary campus. It was so new that almost no one was familiar with all the stairs and doorways behind the stage. When it was time for us graduates to head for the platform, we lined up behind a person who thought he knew where he was going. It was taking us a while to navigate all the stairs and doors when suddenly our leader came to an abrupt halt causing us to plow into each other and knocking some of us over like dominoes. The problem? He had led us not out to the stage entrance but directly into the baptistry. Fortunately there was no water in it, but a few in the audience had seen our unplanned excursion and they, along with us, began to laugh. By the time we had all backed up in the narrow hallway, gone through the correct door, and found our seats on the platform, we were really laughing, some of us uncontrollably. At least that graduation got off to a very happy start.

As you read this final chapter, you might assume that you have reached the conclusion of your study on renewing your mind. The truth, however, is that this is really the beginning. Just as graduation ceremonies are often called commencement exercises because they mark the beginning of a new life for the graduates, these final pages of this study are hopefully the opening lines of a new and happy chapter in your life. You may be reading these pages as a young person at the beginning of your life or as one who has many years of experience behind you. In either case, my hope is that this marks for you the beginning of a life of renewed thinking.

The Content of Renewed Thinking

As we saw earlier, what you think determines who you will become. *Proper thinking* is a prerequisite for *positive living*. Let's take a look now at what the apostle Paul considers to be proper thinking as described in Philippians 4:8. This one verse is packed with many ideas about the kinds of thoughts that will help renew your mind and transform your life. Here, Paul describes for us the *content* of renewed thinking.

Whatever Is True

Paul begins Philippians 4:8 by encouraging us to think upon *"whatever is true."* There are many ideas in this world that are not true, though many people might claim they are. Some people also have the mistaken notion that if enough people believe something, it must be true. However, we have seen time and again that something people thought to be true has been proven to be false. For example, for centuries people believed that the earth was flat until Greek scholars proposed that it might be round. Eventually mankind was able to accumulate many overwhelming evidences to prove that the earth indeed is round.

There is, however, one place where we will always discover truth: God's Word. Jesus prays in John 17:17, "Sanctify them by the truth; your word is truth." We are told in John 1:14, that Jesus is "full of grace and truth." Jesus Himself said in John 14:6, "I am the way and the truth and the life. No one comes to the Father except through me."

According to Psalm 119:160, the Word of God is truth, and Jesus applied that directly to us when He stated, "You will know the truth, and the truth will set you free" (John 8:32). Then there are Paul's words to Timothy:

> Keep reminding them of these things. Warn them before God against quarreling about words; it is of no value, and only ruins those who listen. Do your best to present yourself to God as one approved, a workman who does not need to be ashamed and who correctly handles the word of truth (2 Timothy 2:14-15).

The emphasis here is that we are not to waste our time with "godless chatter" (verse 16) but to concentrate on that which is true. Now we need to keep in mind that Satan seldom presents us with a blatantly untruthful temptation. He knows we would recognize its origin. Rather, he deceives by presenting borderline suggestions that distract us from the truth. The more we know Christ and the Scriptures, the more we will have trained ourselves "to distinguish good from evil,"[1] and we will find ourselves freed[2] by the truth. Only those things which are true will be effective for renewing our minds in a world filled with deception.

Whatever Is Noble

Next, Paul encourages us to think about *"whatever is noble."* These words speak of that which is worthy of honor or reverence—just the opposite of that which is flippant or dishonorable. Many of the situation comedies on television today make light of what are actually serious subjects. While at times we need to laugh at ourselves and our actions, we want to make sure we don't carry this too far. When we take the good things that God has given us and make a farce out of them, we place ourselves on thin ice.

Do you remember the last time you watched one of those programs and found yourself laughing at what would be considered inappropriate or coarse humor? Possibly you were as shocked, as I myself have been, to realize what you were chuckling about. It really wasn't funny at all; it was down right dishonorable! Renewed thinking will help you to focus upon honorable things. In God's Word, we learn a great deal about Him and His works, all of which are worthy of our meditation.

Whatever Is Right

The next phrase, *"whatever is right,"* is self-explanatory. We're to think about whatever is right or virtuous for us as Christians. Something may be right but not suitable for a certain situation; therefore, right thinking includes proper timing. Dr. Radmacher gives us helpful insight when he discusses right thinking; he suggests that "right thinking about God is the logical place to begin."[3] He continues:

I realize, of course, that humanists would object, insisting that we must study man himself if we are going to understand man and his world. But humanists will never open the door to a true understanding of the nature of man without the only key to that door. The key is knowing what God is like. So the proper study of man is not man; the proper study of man is God.[4]

Certain things are right and others are not. If we meditate upon the wrongs of life, we will be fearful, discouraged, critical people. But if "whatever is right" becomes the input for our mental computers, the result will be right thinking and living.

Whatever Is Pure

The apostle Paul says to think on that *"whatever is pure."* James' words are parallel to those of Paul at this point: "Come near to God and he will come near to you. Wash your hands, you sinners, and purify your hearts, you double-minded" (James 4:8). It is God's design that the Christian mind be constantly fed by pure thoughts. The weight of Scripture is overwhelming on this subject. James challenges us not to be "double-minded," trying to live like a Christian and, at the same time, live like the world. To be pure is to be "ceremonially cleansed from defilement."[5] We are to think undefiled thoughts and thereby display pure actions.

Some of us are under the mistaken impression we can entertain impure thoughts and still live a moral life. That is impossible! The root of the tree ultimately determines its fruit. If the root is rotten, the fruit will reveal it.[6] Pure thinking will affect our relationship with God,[7] with fellow Christians,[8] and our daily lives as we look forward to Christ's return.[9]

As an experiment you might take today's newspaper or choose a favorite television show and list all of the items that convey or suggest impure ideas and events as compared with those which prompt pure thinking. Make this a family project so the children can have a part in discovering this truth. I believe you will be amazed at the results.

Whatever Is Lovely

Paul further exhorts us to dwell on *"whatever is lovely."* In the original Greek text, the word lovely refers to that which is pleasing. It is something that draws love out of the heart. To some, a garden of colorful flowers is lovely; to others, a sunset or rainbow is a vision to behold. Lovely thoughts center upon things that call out a response of love and beauty. We don't need to stretch our necks very far to find the opposite. Simply turn on your television; and at any hour, you can hear of hatred, deception, sexual wrongdoing, violence, and tragedy. Somehow we have been led to believe we are not properly informed if we do not see life as it "really is." Newspaper publishers and television programmers tell us this is what people want. It may be true that many people crave this perverted fare, but as a believer in Christ, our interests in life are radically altered. Although we may read and watch to keep up on the news of the world around us, we must be careful to filter what enters our thinking and determine to respond to it according to God's Word. We do not need to feed upon the base things of life. To be transformed, we need to dwell on those things which are lovely. The result of this kind of thinking is Christlikeness. Unlovely things call forth anger, bitterness, and lust. Lovely things help us to become "conformed to the likeness of his Son" (Romans 8:29).

What is our source for this kind of meditation? The answer is obvious. We will discover that which is lovely and beautiful in God's Word and His character. As the songwriter said, "He is altogether lovely."

Whatever Is Admirable

Last in Paul's list of the contents of renewed thinking is *"whatever is admirable."* When a person has a good reputation, other people speak well of that individual. His life is seen as admirable. In the same way, there are thoughts and ideas that have good reputations.

If all of your thoughts were projected on a screen above your head, how would those around you respond to them? Would your innermost thoughts, if known, be admirable? God's thoughts are always reputable and they are available to us in His Word. And His Word is so rich that we could never exhaust all that is accessible to us by way of admirable thoughts.

Whatever Is Excellent or Praiseworthy

Paul then says, *"If anything is excellent or praiseworthy—think about such things"* (Philippians 4:8). Paul's list is not inclusive of every excellent matter worthy of praise; his suggestions are only the beginnings of renewed thinking. The Word of God is filled with other excellent truths that are food for thought.

Now, this is where we must make a choice. You can sit at a table spread with every type of delicious food, but you will receive no benefit from it until you eat it. In the same way, you may have at your disposal all the priceless truths of God's Word but your mind will never be renewed unless you "think about such things." Not just once or occasionally, but repeatedly. We need to make use of memorization, meditation, and imagination.

Every hour of the day, we need to choose the kinds of thoughts we will entertain, and our choices determine the quality of our lives.

From Renewed Thinking
to Renewed Living

The apostle Paul concluded his challenge by saying,

> Whatever you have learned or received or heard from me, or seen in me—put it into practice. And the God of peace will be with you (Philippians 4:9).

Learning is more than acquiring knowledge. It results in a true *change of behavior*. We can know that we have truly learned what it means to renew our minds when we *apply* that knowledge and see positive changes taking place in our lives. Have you been putting into practice that which you have read? Let's look again at what's involved in the process of renewing our minds.

1. *Information*—from God's Word

2. *Memorization*—hiding it in your heart so it is available when needed

3. *Meditation*—reflecting on the truth throughout your waking hours to derive all its nutrients

4. *Imagination*—seeing yourself obeying God's principles

5. *Application*—putting the principles to work in your everyday life

You now have all the tools for a changed mind. However, you must do what Paul said and "put it into practice" if you want to experience a changed life.

Do you have a Christian friend who would be willing to help you apply these principles? One of the purposes of the church is that God's people are to gather to "spur one another on toward love and good deeds" (Hebrews 10:24). Find another believer who desires to have a new mind and covenant together to encourage one another and hold each other accountable for growth. Your example will become a strong testimony for others to follow, and the principles of renewed thinking will be seen in your life.

The Consequence of Renewed Thinking

Paul says that when we put all this into practice, "the God of peace will be with you" (Philippians 4:9). The Scriptures speak repeatedly of positive results that will be yours if you are thinking God's way. Romans 12:1-2 promises you will have a renewed mind and a transformed life. Earlier in this book, we also learned that through mind renewal you can develop a proper self-image (Romans 12:3-5), experience victory over sin (Luke 4:1-13), learn to cope with stress (Philippians 4:4-6), and prosper in whatever you do (Psalm 1:3).

Your family, business, and school life as well as all your interpersonal relationships will be affected in a positive way. Your Christian witness will be strengthened, and you will enjoy true peace and contentment.

Finally, when we allow God to transform us by the renewing of the mind, we allow Him to accomplish His ultimate purpose in our lives:

> Those God foreknew he also predestined to be conformed to the likeness of his Son, that he might be the firstborn among many brothers (Romans 8:29).

You may remember that in an earlier discussion, I suggested that the word "conformed" used here is the same as the word "transformed" in Romans 12:2. Our being conformed to Christ's image or likeness is the end result of submitting to God's transforming work in this life. Some Christians might assume that while we are here on earth, we must live with all of the challenges of a world full of sin and cannot experience any of the benefits of transformation until we arrive in heaven. However, we can enjoy the fruit of transformation right now!

It Began in the Garden

For a moment, let's go back to the beginning as God has revealed it in Genesis. In a discussion within the Godhead—the Father, the Son, and the Holy Spirit—God said, "Let us make man in our image, in our likeness" (Genesis 1:26). We then read that God created man in His own image, "in the image of God he created him; male and female he created them" (Genesis 1:27).

God's original design was, amazingly, for us to *be like him*. That doesn't mean we become God or even little gods, but rather, that there are attributes that we share with God. Although there is much controversy as to what the image of God in man actually is, it would be logical, I believe, that it has nothing to do with physical attributes because God is Spirit and does not have a body,[10] even though later, God the Son would take on flesh and dwell among us.[11]

I believe it is safe to assume that the "image" as described in Genesis referred to mind, will, and emotion. Undoubtedly God has many attributes that are reserved for Him alone, such as His omnipotence and omniscience. There are, however, many attributes we possess that are similar to His. However, when sin entered the world as recorded in Genesis chapter 3, great damage was done to this image or likeness. Although the image was not lost entirely, it was drastically marred, which resulted in all of us being born into sin, hopelessly lost apart from Christ.[12]

I personally believe that when Romans 8:29 describes Christ as the "firstborn among many brothers," it speaks not only of His completed work on the cross for the remission of our sins, but also of His leading the way to perfect humanity when He was resurrected and ascended into heaven to be seated at the Father's right hand.[13]

As Christians, we now are to be conformed to the image of God's Son, Jesus. We are to become like Him in every way. Although the final transformation will not take place until we "see him as he is,"[14] the process began when we became saved and continues until we are finally glorified.[15] That process is described in 2 Corinthians 3:18, where we read:

> We all, with unveiled face beholding as in a mirror the glory of the Lord, are being transformed into the same image from glory to glory, just as from the Lord, the Spirit (NASB).

Living in the Present Tense

Some Christians seem to confuse the tenses of their lives. Certainly we are to have our eyes on the future tense, when we will be "caught up . . . to meet the Lord in the air . . . and be with the Lord forever" (1 Thessalonians 4:17), but we are to live in the present tense. Even Jesus himself teaches us to live one day at time.[16]

Yet what may well be one of the most exciting truths about the Christian life is that we don't need to wait until we get to heaven to become more like Christ. It's not necessary for us to only hope for some future date when we will be transformed. Transformation and all its accompanying blessings can be a part of our lives today!

Well, What Do You Think?

Well, what do you think? That is an important question to consider, for what you think determines who you will become. The potential of a new mind and a transformed life is exciting!

If you have begun applying the guidelines shared in this book, you are already on your way to changing your mind and life. Don't stop now! And if you have not yet begun, don't put down this book without making a decision to begin. Your determination to renew your mind will revolutionize your life and will finally bring about the kind of change you long for—a complete transformation into Christlikeness. This is *your* commencement!

Prayer

Father, thank You for the challenge of Your Word concerning the renewal of my mind. I know I cannot succeed in this process apart from Your power. Please challenge me to step out in faith and become the person You want me to be, conformed to the likeness of your Son. I know "I can do everything through [Christ] who gives me strength" (Philippians 4:13). In the name of Christ, amen.

Bible Verses for Everyday Living

Below are some categories of Bible verses that are applicable to various circumstances we are likely to encounter in life. With the help of this list, you'll be able to find the Bible's *information* in areas of interest to you. This is not an exhaustive list, but is intended to help provide some starting points from which you can begin to make Scripture the guide for renewing your mind.

ANXIETY
Psalm 37:4-5
Isaiah 26:3
Isaiah 40:28-31
Matthew 6:25-34
Philippians 4:4-7
1 Peter 5:7

BITTERNESS
Ephesians 4:31
Hebrews 12:14-15

CHASTENING
Proverbs 3:11-12
Hebrews 12:5-6,11

COMFORT
Romans 15:4
2 Corinthians 1:3-4
Philippians 4:19
2 Thessalonians 2:16-17

CONFESSION OF SIN
Psalm 32:1-5
Psalm 51:2,10-12
Psalm 139:23-24
1 John 1:8-10

DISCOURAGEMENT
Joshua 1:9
Matthew 11:28-30
Romans 8:28
Galatians 6:9

DOUBT
Mark 9:24
Mark 10:27
Romans 4:20
2 Timothy 2:13
Hebrews 10:35-38
Hebrews 11:6

FASTING
Matthew 6:16-18

FEAR
Psalm 46:1-3
Matthew 6:27
Matthew 10:28
Luke 12:4-5
2 Timothy 1:7
Hebrews 13:6
1 John 4:18

FORGIVING OTHERS
Matthew 6:14-15
Matthew 18:21-35
Mark 11:25
John 8:7

GIVING
Proverbs 3:9-10
Proverbs 11:24-25
Malachi 3:10
Matthew 6:1-4
Luke 6:38
2 Corinthians 9:6-7

HONESTY
Isaiah 33:15-16
1 Peter 2:12

HUMILITY
Proverbs 8:13
Proverbs 16:5
Proverbs 16:18
Matthew 23:12
Philippians 2:3
Colossians 3:22-24
James 4:6,10
1 Peter 5:5-6

INDULGENCE
Psalm 69:5
Mark 8:36-37
Romans 6:12
Romans 14:23
1 Corinthians 6:19-20
1 Corinthians 10:31
2 Corinthians 12:9
Galatians 5:16
1 John 2:16

JUDGING OTHERS
Matthew 7:1-5
Luke 6:37
Romans 14:13

MATERIALISM
Isaiah 55:1-3
Matthew 6:19-24
Matthew 16:24-27
Mark 8:34-37
Luke 9:23-25
Luke 12:29-31,34
Luke 16:13
Philippians 3:7-8
Philippians 4:11
Colossians 3:1-3
1 Timothy 6:6-11
Hebrews 13:5
1 John 2:15-17

PERSECUTION
Matthew 5:10-12
Romans 12:14,18-21
2 Timothy 2:3
1 Peter 2:19-23

PRAYER
Matthew 7:7-11
Matthew 21:21-22
Mark 11:23-24
Luke 18:1-8
John 14:13-14
John 16:23-24
Ephesians 6:18
1 Thessalonians 5:17-18
Hebrews 4:16
James 4:3
1 John 3:18-23

1 John 5:14-15

PROMISE OF CHRIST'S RETURN
Matthew 24:42
Matthew 25:13
Mark 13:24-27
1 Corinthians 15:51-52
1 Thessalonians 4:16-18
2 Peter 3:10-11
1 John 2:28–3:3
Revelation 1:7

PURE LIVING
Matthew 5:8
1 Thessalonians 4:1-8
1 Timothy 4:12
2 Timothy 2:19-22
James 4:8
1 Peter 1:14-16
1 Peter 3:12
1 John 2:28–3:3

PURE THOUGHTS
Proverbs 12:5
Mark 7:20-23
2 Corinthians 10:5
Philippians 4:8-9
Hebrews 4:12

RELATIONSHIPS WITH OTHERS
Psalm 41:1
Matthew 5:38-44
Luke 6:27-31
Romans 12:10
Galatians 5:13-15
Galatians 6:10
Ephesians 4:25-32
Hebrews 13:16

James 2:8-9
1 John 3:18

SEPARATION—HUMAN LOSS
Isaiah 25:8
Matthew 5:4
John 14:1-3
1 Corinthians 15:50-57
1 Thessalonians 4:13-14

SUFFERING—TRIBULATION
Romans 8:18,28
James 1:2-3,12
1 Peter 1:6-7
1 Peter 4:12-16
1 Peter 5:8-10

TEMPER
Proverbs 14:29
Proverbs 15:1
Romans 12:17-21
Ephesians 4:26-27
James 1:19-20

TEMPTATION
Luke 4:1-13
1 Corinthians 10:13
James 1:13-15
1 Peter 1:6-7

TONGUE
Psalm 34:13
Psalm 141:3

Proverbs 13:3
Matthew 15:18
Romans 14:10-13
Ephesians 4:25-26,29-31
James 1:26
James 3:5-11
1 Peter 3:10

VICTORY
2 Corinthians 1:9-10
2 Corinthians 2:14
2 Corinthians 3:5
2 Corinthians 12:9-10
Galatians 2:20
Ephesians 3:20
Philippians 4:13
Hebrews 12:1-2

WEARINESS
Isaiah 40:29-31
Matthew 11:28-30
1 Corinthians 15:58
Galatians 6:9
2 Thessalonians 3:13
Hebrews 12:1-3

WITNESSING
Matthew 5:13-16
Matthew 10:16-23,32-33
Matthew 28:18-20
Luke 12:8-9
John 13:34-35
2 Corinthians 5:17-21
Colossians 4:5-6

Study Guide

Chapter 1—Changing the Way You Think and Live

1. Review the questions asked on pages 25-26. Can you respond favorably to all of them? Why or why not?

2. A eulogy is a speech praising a person who has recently died. Write a eulogy for yourself in 50 words or less. What would you be remembered for in the areas of family, work, character, faith, and general accomplishments?

3. Give your own definition of the "heart" as described in Scripture.

4. Read Proverbs 3:1-6 and then answer the following questions:

a. What does it mean to keep the commands *in* your heart? (verse 1). What benefits will there be in doing so (verse 2)?

b. How does one write love and faithfulness *on* the tablet of their heart? (verse 3). What benefits result from doing this? (verse 4).

c. Describe a situation in which you have trusted the Lord with all your heart.

5. Read Proverbs 23:6-8. Explain what you believe verse 7 means and how it would apply to your life.

6. In what two or three areas of your life do you desire to be transformed?

Action Steps

1. Memorize 2 Corinthians 3:18.

2. During the next week, ask God to help you become aware of where you receive most of the input for your thought life. Is it from television, newspapers, teachers, friends, radio, the internet, or . . . ? At the end of the week, evaluate the percentage of your time that goes to those various sources of input. In what areas could you make changes for the better?

Chapter 2—Releasing the Captive

1. Review the memory verse from the last chapter, 2 Corinthians 3:18.

2. Do a study of the Bible passages that describe Satan's methods of tempting and deceiving two well-known individuals, answering the questions listed below:

a. Eve—Genesis 3:1-7

   1) How did Satan approach Eve?

   2) What tactics did he use to deceive her? How did she respond?

   3) How did he use God's Word?

   4) Are there parallels between Satan's tempta-tion of Eve and the description of worldliness in 1 John 2:15-17 (especially verse 16)? List some of the similarities.

b. David—2 Samuel 11

1) Read the chapter, noting David's progression toward sin.

2) How did David set himself up for sin?

3) What was his response to his sin?

4) What were the immediate consequences?

5) Are there any similarities between Eve's temptation and David's?

3. Read the following passages and describe Satan's strategies:

   a. 2 Corinthians 2:10-11: What are some of Satan's schemes?

   b. 2 Corinthians 4:3-4: How does Satan blind unbelievers?

   c. 2 Corinthians 11:3: What are some ways he leads us astray from a pure devotion to Christ?

   d. 2 Corinthians 11:14: How does he disguise himself in our experiences?

4. List the three weapons of warfare listed in chapter two that we are given to resist Satan. Then describe

how you might use them in your struggles with temptation. Try to give specific examples.

Action Steps

1. Memorize Colossians 3:2.

2. Keep a diary of your temptations. Ask God's Spirit to show you when temptation comes. Write down the specific instances throughout the week.

3. Read Colossians 3:1-4 at least once each day in the coming week. Consider your mindset. What do you most often think about during the day? Record your findings.

Chapter 3—Recapturing Your Thoughts

1. Review the memory verses 2 Corinthians 3:18 and Colossians 3:2.

2. Answer the following questions:

   a. What do people most often set their minds upon? Make a list.

   b. From what sources do we receive the input that forms our mindset? If you did the second action step at the end of the study guide questions for chapter 1 (see page 188), then use that list to help answer this question.

3. Make a list of the ten things you desire most (material, spiritual, physical, and so on).

   a.

   b.

c.

d.

e.

f.

g.

h.

i.

j.

4. Read the following Scriptures and record your findings:

   a. *Romans 8:1-17*

      1) What contrasts are used?

      2) What are the results of the two different mind-sets— flesh and spirit?

   b. *Matthew 16:21-23*

      1) Why did Peter react so strongly to Christ's words? What was his motivation?

      2) Why did Jesus rebuke Peter so firmly? What can we learn from His rebuke?

c. *Philippians 3:17-19*

  1) Whose example should we follow?

  2) Why are some people enemies of the cross?

  3) What demonstrates that a person's mind is set on earthly things?

5. Return to your "Ten Most Desired" list and do the following:

  a. Place one of the following letters after each item:

    M = Something for *M*yself
    O = Something for *O*thers
    C = Something for *C*hrist

  b. Now place one of the following letters after each desired item to indicate whether it reveals a fleshly or a spiritual mindset.

    F = *F*leshly mindset
    S = *S*piritual mindset

Action Steps

1. Memorize Romans 12:1-2.

2. Practice the four steps in chapter three—*recognize, recapture, refuse,* and *replace*—in an area of your thought life that is a struggle for you. Journal the results of your efforts.

Chapter 4—Choices That Bring Change

1. Review the memory verses for this week, Romans 12:1-2.

2. What is the difference between "conform" and "transformed" in Romans 12:2?

3. For each of the following sections of the book of Ecclesiastes, answer these three questions: What was Solomon's pursuit? What were the results? How might his experience apply to us?

   a. 1:1-11

   b. 1:12-18; 2:12-26

   c. 2:1-11

d. 5:1-9

e. 5:10-17

f. 6:1-12

4. How does Solomon apply his discoveries in Ecclesiastes 12:1,13-14? What can we learn from his challenge?

5. Will you choose to cross the bridge from conformity to consecration? If your answer is yes, you may want to sign the Personal Growth Contract (see next page) to help you to confirm your decision.

Personal Growth Contract

In response to the challenge of Romans 12:1-2, I now give myself as a living sacrifice and commit myself to no longer being conformed to the world, but rather, to becoming transformed by the renewing of my mind.

In the power of the Holy Spirit, I will begin the process by doing the following:

- _____

- _____

- _____

- _____

- _____

- _____

- _____

Signed _____

Action Steps

1. Memorize 2 Timothy 3:16-17. Review 2 Corinthians 3:18; Colossians 3:2; Romans 12:1-2.

2. Over the next few days, ask God's Spirit to make you observant about how often you are tempted to conform to the priorities, pursuits, and pressures of the world. Record here or in a personal journal some of the areas in which you are most often tempted.

Chapter 5—Building on the Rock: *Information*

1. With your Bible closed, read the following questions and list all the Scripture references you can remember that apply to each situation. Briefly describe how the passages relate to the situation.

   a. A young Christian friend of yours says he is considering marriage to a very nice non-Christian woman. He wants your insight concerning his plans. How would you counsel him?

   b. Your next-door neighbor's husband is very ill, and they have almost no income. She tells you she wants to trust God, but she is overcome with anxiety. How would you help her from God's Word?

2. If the government became repressive and outlawed Bibles and yours was taken away, how

much of God's Word do you believe you could reconstruct from memory?

3. What are the three steps of inductive Bible study? List them and briefly describe each one.

   a.

   b.

   c.

4. Study 2 Timothy 3:16-17, using the inductive study method with the help of the questions below:

   a. What do these verses say?

b. What do they mean?

c. How do they apply to you? List some applications.

Action Step

Over the next week study Psalm 1, using the inductive study method. Each time you read it, record your observations, interpretations, and applications.

Chapter 6—What's Gotten Into You?: *Memorization*

1. Is memorization easy or difficult for you?

2. When people say they can't memorize Scripture, what are some of the reasons and excuses they give?

3. Study John 15:1-11 and answer the following questions:

   a. Why do you think Jesus uses the example of the vine and branches?

   b. According to verse 3, what effect does God's Word have on us?

c. How would you explain the idea of "abiding" or "remaining" in the vine (verses 4-6)?

d. What benefit is there to having God's Word remain in us (verse 7)?

e. How does God's Word remain or abide in us?

f. What is the appropriate response to God's Word (verse 10)?

g. What is the result of obedience to the Word (verse 11)?

Action Steps

1. Make a commitment to regularly memorize God's Word.

2. Using one or more of the methods described in chapter six, begin to memorize Psalm 1. Ask someone to hold you accountable.

Chapter 7—Success Unlimited: *Meditation*

1. Quote as much of Psalm 1 from memory as you can.

2. Write down your personal definition of *meditation.*

3. Using Psalm 1 and Joshua 1:7-8, describe what biblical meditation is and mention some of the personal benefits that are promised to those who meditate.

4. Choose either a daydream that often comes to mind or a worry that regularly enters your thinking and describe what goes on in your mind while that thought is present. What triggers the thought? What feeds it? How does it take shape?

What physical or emotional responses does it elicit? How often does the thought surface?

5. What makes biblical meditation difficult for you? What would need to change in your life, schedule, or commitments for biblical meditation to become a regular part of your life?

Action Steps

1. Take time over a period of days to meditate on Psalm 1. Continue your memorization of the psalm as well.

2. Do you have an area of temptation that is a regular struggle (for example worry, lust, fear)? Using the pattern from chapter three—*recognize, recapture, refuse,* and *replace*—take Psalm 1 and meditate upon it in place of thoughts concerning your area of weakness. Follow the pattern every time the tempting thought occurs.

Chapter 8—Imagine That!: *Imagination*

1. Read 1 Chronicles 28:9, then answer the following questions:

   a. What does it mean to acknowledge and serve God with wholehearted devotion?

   b. How does a person develop a willing mind?

   c. The word "motive" in 1 Chronicles 28:9 could be translated "imagination." How do you feel about God examining your imagination?

    d. Would you be willing to have the contents of your imagination projected on a screen for others to see? Why or why not?

    e. How can our imagination aid in seeking God?

2. Imagine that you have been given $100,000 to spend with the only stipulation being that it must be spent within 24 hours. Using your imagination, record how you would use the money and why.

3. What areas of your imagination are most troubling to you? Why? What areas are most beneficial? Why? If you could change any facet of your imagination, what would it be?

Action Steps

1. Choose a situation that you expect will occur in the next week (interview, witnessing opportunity, meeting with someone, etc.) and, using your imagination, picture how you will respond, what you will say, and what you will do. Write down your imagined scenario.

2. Where does your imagination most often deviate from biblical guidelines? In the coming hours, begin using God's Word to reprogram your imagination. Discover the appropriate information, memorize it, meditate on it regularly, and then make God's truth the content of your imagination as a replacement for the faulty information.

Chapter 9—Buried Treasure: *Application*

1. Let's review the key principles for renewing our minds by answering the following questions:

   a. What is important about the *information* we put in our minds? What difference does it make where it comes from?

   b. How will *memorization* affect my thinking and living? How many of the assigned memory verses can I recite now?

   c. What does *meditation* do for a person's mind? What content is most beneficial for meditation?

   d. How does a person's *imagination* relate to the process of renewing the mind? Can a person hold onto evil imaginations and still be renewed?

2. Now, tie the steps to mind renewal together by doing the following concerning *application*:

a. What did Jesus' parable of the two builders in Matthew 7:24-27 emphasize in regard to the importance of application?

b. What does Jesus say in John 13:17 about application?

c. Read Joshua 1:6-9. How does God emphasize application to Joshua?

Action Steps

1. Now that you have read chapters 5–9, which explain the five steps to mind renewal, do the following:

   a. Review your personal growth contract in chapter 4.

   b. How have you done in following through?

   c. What changes do you believe you should make in light of chapters 5–9?

2. Memorize and meditate upon John 13:17.

Chapter 10—Who's Who in You?

1. How important do you believe a proper self-image is? Why?

2. Read Numbers 13:17-33 and answer the following questions:

   a. How did the ten spies view themselves?

   b. How did they view God?

   c. How did Joshua and Caleb view themselves?

   d. Read Numbers 13:30. How did Joshua and Caleb view God?

e. Do we ever view ourselves as grasshoppers? Why?

3. What is the world's view of an ideal person?

4. What is necessary so that we can see ourselves from God's perspective? What is His ideal for us?

5. Using Genesis 1:26-31 and 2 Corinthians 5:11-21, record some of the biblical information about our value as individuals created by God and redeemed by Christ.

Action Steps

1. Memorize Romans 12:3 and 2 Corinthians 5:17.

2. Read the following verses, and write a list of everything you can learn about who you are in Christ:

   John 1:12

   John 15:15

   Romans 8:1

   Romans 8:14-15

   1 Corinthians 1:30

1 Corinthians 6:19-20

1 Corinthians 12:27

2 Corinthians 5:17

Ephesians 1:3-8

Ephesians 2:10

1 Peter 2:9-10

Chapter 11—"It Is Written"

1. Read James 1:13-15 and answer the following questions:

   a. What is God's part in temptation?

   b. What is the source of temptation?

   c. What are the steps of the temptation process?

   d. What are the results?

   e. Is temptation itself sin? When does it become sin?

2. Read 1 Corinthians 10:11-13 and respond to the
   following:

   a. Why does God give us Old Testament stories?

   b. What is important about the warning found in
      verse 12?

   c. According to verse 13:

      1) Are any of our temptations original?

      2) How does God demonstrate His faithfulness?

      3) Are any temptations unbearable?

4) In light of what we have been studying, what is the "way out" when we are tempted?

5) What does it mean to "stand up under [temptation]"?

3. What are some biblical references to God's faithfulness in the areas of our temptation such as worry, lust, fear, greed, anger, and so on? In what ways will He be faithful to us in dealing with these temptations?

Action Steps

1. Review the diary in which you record your encounters with temptation (see action steps at the end of the study guide questions for chapter 2). Which of those temptations are the biggest problem for you now?

2. Using the process we have discovered in the earlier chapters, imagine yourself facing that temptation the next time it arises. What steps will you take to prepare for it? What actions will you take as soon as you recognize the temptation? Follow your plan when the temptation comes and record the results.

3. Memorize 1 Corinthians 10:12-13.

Chapter 12—Coping with Constant Confusion

1. Where is there the greatest stress in your life?

    a. How do these stresses affect you physically, spiritually, emotionally?

    b. What have you done in the past to deal with them? Have your efforts been successful?

2. Read Matthew 11:28-30 and answer the following:

    a. What does it mean to be "weary and burdened"?

    b. What do you believe Jesus means by "rest"?

c. What is a yoke used for? How does a yoke relate to rest?

d. Who promises rest? Is any other source offered?

e. What does verse 29 tell us about Jesus' character?

f. How can a yoke be easy and a burden light?

g. What steps would you need to take right now to get into the yoke with Christ?

3. Read Psalm 4:1-8 and answer the following questions:

   a. How does David deal with stress?

   b. What is it that stresses him?

   c. What responses to stress does he encourage? What responses does he discourage?

   d. What is the result of David's turning to God in his times of stress?

Action Steps

   1. Memorize Philippians 4:6-7.

   2. Identify a situation in your life that's placing the greatest stress on you. Develop a plan for handling that stress based upon the principles we have

been learning throughout the book (especially the five steps given in chapters 5–9). Work out your plan over the next few days and record both your successes and failures. What factors will help you to be successful in applying your plan? What factors could cause you to fail to carry out your plan?

Chapter 13—Looking Ahead

1. Read Philippians 4:8 and list one or two examples that come to your mind when you read the following phrases:

   a. Whatever is true:

   b. Whatever is noble:

   c. Whatever is right:

   d. Whatever is pure:

   e. Whatever is lovely:

f. Whatever is admirable:

g. Anything excellent:

h. Anything praiseworthy:

2. How are you doing at setting your mind on such things? Have you made progress in recent days or weeks?

3. Which of the principles that you have been learning have been most helpful to you in the process of renewing your mind?

4. Is there any way in which you think differently now than you did when you began reading this book?

5. While you have finished this book, you are now just beginning to make mind renewal real in your life. What specific changes would you like to see most in your thought life? Set two or three goals and explain how you can best meet those goals in the upcoming weeks.

Action Steps

1. Related to the last question above, set a schedule for routine review of the steps you plan to take to meet your goal, write them down, and put the schedule in a place where you will see it regularly.

2. Take a moment now and commit yourself to an ongoing process of renewing your mind and seeing your life transformed into Christlikeness.

Notes

Chapter 1—Changing the Way You Think and Live

1. See also 2 Corinthians 3:2-3.
2. Mark 7:1-17.
3. John R.W. Stott, *Your Mind Matters* (Leicester, England: InterVarsity Press, 1972), p. 41. Used by permission of InterVarsity Press, P.O. Box 1400, Downers Grove, IL 60515.
4. 2 Corinthians 3:16; Romans 10:9-10; John 1:12; Acts 4:12.
5. Hebrews 4:12.
6. Robert Boyd Munger, *My Heart—Christ's Home* (Downers Grove, IL: InterVarsity Press, 1986).

Chapter 2—Releasing the Captive

1. Isaiah 14:12-15; Ezekiel 28:15-17.
2. E.M. Bounds, *The Weapon of Prayer* (Grand Rapids, MI: Baker Book House, 1975), p. 9.
3. Hebrews 4:16.
4. 2 Corinthians 2:11.
5. 2 Corinthians 10:4-5.
6. John 8:44.
7. Earl D. Radmacher, *You and Your Thoughts* (Wheaton, IL: Tyndale House Publishers, Inc., 1977), p. 61.
8. Hebrews 12:15.
9. 2 Corinthians 10:5.
10. See Proverbs 1:20-33.

11. 2 Timothy 2:2-7.
12. Philippians 4:8.

Chapter 3—Recapturing Your Thoughts

1. 2 Corinthians 10:5.
2. Matthew 6:25-34.
3. Ephesians 4:26.
4. Ephesians 4:32.
5. 2 Timothy 1:7.
6. 2 Timothy 2:22.
7. Colossians 3:2.
8. Philippians 3:20.

Chapter 4—Choices That Bring Change

1. Brother Lawrence, *The Practice of the Presence of God* (Old Tappan, NJ: Fleming H. Revell Co., 1958).
2. Acts 16:31.
3. Romans 12:1.
4. J.B. Phillips, *The New Testament in Modern English* (London: Geoffrey Bles, 1960), p. 332.
5. Ecclesiastes 12:8.
6. 2 Corinthians 7:8-11.

Chapter 5—Building on the Rock: Information

1. Luke 15:11-31.
2. 2 Peter 1:3.

Chapter 6—What's Gotten into You?: Memorization

1. Jeremiah 29:12-14.
2. Psalm 119:10.
3. Psalm 106:7.
4. Psalm 106:13.
5. Deuteronomy 8:1-20.
6. Jerry Lucas, *Ready—Set—Remember* (White's Creek, TN: Memory Press, Inc., The Benson Co., 1978), p. 7.
7. Ibid.
8. Deuteronomy 6:7.
9. Ephesians 5:15-16.

Chapter 7—Success Unlimited: Meditation

1. J.I. Packer, *Knowing God* (Downers Grove, IL: InterVarsity Press, 1973), pp. 18-19. Used by permission.
2. *How to Reflect on The Word of God: A Primer on Meditation* (Colorado Springs: NavPress), p. 6.
3. Ecclesiastes 2:9,11.
4. 1 Timothy 6:6.
5. 1 Timothy 4:12-15.
6. Joshua 1:8.
7. 2 Peter 1:3.
8. David F. Wells, "Musing on God's Ways," *Christianity Today*, September 20, 1972.
9. Malcolm Smith, *How Christians Meditate* (NJ: Logos International, 1977), p. 7.
10. Ibid., p. 6.
11. Luke 6:12.
12. Psalm 77:12 (NASB).
13. Psalm 145:5.
14. Romans 1:20.
15. Romans 1:25.
16. 2 Peter 1:2-4.
17. Psalm 119:15,27,99,148.
18. Psalm 1:2.
19. Psalm 63:6.
20. Psalm 119:97.
21. David F. Wells, "Musing on God's Ways," *Christianity Today*.
22. Psalm 1:3.

Chapter 8—Imagine That!: Imagination

1. Proverbs 23:7.
2. Ronald B. Allen, *Imagination* (Portland, OR: Multnomah Press, 1985), p. 5.
3. Ezekiel 8:12.
4. Os Guinness, *No God But God: Breaking with the Idols of Our Age* (Chicago: Moody Press, 1992), pp. 24-25.
5. Psalm 73:7 (NASB).
6. Ephesians 5:15-16.
7. Malcolm Smith, *How Christians Meditate* (NJ: Logos International, 1977), pp. 20-21.

8. Stephen Charnock, *The Existence and Attributes of God,* vol. 1 (Grand Rapids: Baker Book House, 1979), p. 11.
9. Joseph Henry Thayer, D.D., *A Greek-English Lexicon of the New Testament* (New York: American Book Co., 1889), p. 579.
10. Ronald B. Allen, *Imagination*, pp. 5-6.
11. Joseph Henry Thayer, D.D., *A Greek-English Lexicon of the New Testament*, p. 224.
12. Romans 8:29.

Chapter 9—Buried Treasure: Application

1. John R.W. Stott, *Your Mind Matters* (Leicester, England: InterVarsity Press, 1972), p. 57. Used by permission of InterVarsity Press, P.O. Box 1400, Downers Grove, IL 60515.
2. Ibid., p. 56.
3. Deuteronomy 6:1.
4. James 1:22 (NASB).
5. Matthew 5–7.

Chapter 10—Who's Who in You?

1. Maxwell Maltz, *Psycho-cybernetics* (Hollywood: Wilshire Book Company, 1960), p. 2.
2. Dr. James Dobson, *Hide or Seek* (Old Tappan, NJ: Fleming H. Revell, 1974), p. 150.
3. 1 Samuel 16:7
4. Proverbs 3:34; James 4:6; 1 Peter 5:5-6.
5. Dr. James Dobson, *Hide or Seek*, p. 26.
6. Ibid., p. 27.
7. Don Matzat, *Christ Esteem* (Eugene, OR: Harvest House Publishers, 1990), p. 92.
8. Romans 8:29.
9. 1 Corinthians 12:7; 14:12.

Chapter 11—"It Is Written"

1. 1 Corinthians 10:13.
2. Genesis 3:1-7.
3. 2 Corinthians 4:4 (NASB).
4. 2 Corinthians 11:3.
5. Psalm 91:11-12.
6. James 4:7.

7. Hebrews 12:1.
8. 1 Thessalonians 4:3-5.
9. 1 Corinthians 10:13.

Chapter 12—Coping with Constant Confusion

1. Dr. Gary Collins, *You Can Profit from Stress* (Santa Ana, CA: Vision House Publishers, 1977), p. 13.
2. Philippians 4:8 (NASB).

Chapter 13—Looking Ahead

1. Hebrews 5:14.
2. John 8:32.
3. Earl D. Radmacher, *You and Your Thoughts* (Wheaton, IL: Tyndale House, 1977), p. 34.
4. Ibid., p. 34.
5. Abbott-Smith, *A Manual Greek Lexicon of the New Testament* (New York: Charles Scribner's Sons, 1939), p. 6.
6. Matthew 7:15-20.
7. James 4:7-8.
8. 1 Peter 1:22.
9. 1 John 3:2-3.
10. John 4:24.
11. John 1:14.
12. Romans 3:10-20.
13. See Hebrews 2:6-18; 4:14–5:10; Colossians 3:1-4.
14. 1 John 3:2.
15. Romans 8:30.
16. Matthew 6:25-34.

Other Good
Harvest House Reading

A Passion for God
Greg Laurie

Evangelist Greg Laurie explores the dynamic faith and experiences of the early church and discovers what these believers did to turn their world upside down. Packed with practical applications and specific action steps, *A Passion for God* shows you how to tap into the powerhouse of spiritual revival, ignite a bonfire of passion for serving the Lord, and erect a foundation of faith that can withstand persecution and trials.

Pathway to the Heart of God
Terry Glaspey

Have you ever wondered what C.S. Lewis, A.W. Tozer, and Corrie ten Boom felt about prayer? Terry Glaspey's insightful narrative weaves together inspiring thoughts on the wonder and power of communion with God, resulting in a stirring journey to the very heart of God.

Meeting God in Holy Places
F. LaGard Smith

See one Bible story after another come vividly to life through the eyes of the author. Touch the stones in the valley where David slew the mighty Goliath. Visit the Pool of Bethesda and feel the healing power of Christ. Be near Jesus in Gethsemane. These captivating devotionals are graced by English artist Glenda Rae's masterful watercolor paintings of the Holy Land.

God's Best for My Life
Lloyd John Ogilvie

This perennial inspirational favorite gives you daily devotionals to help you discover the power and beauty of a Christ-centered life, encouraging you to travel the path to true discipleship and discover the joy of serving Jesus Christ every day.